*Intimate
Portraits
of the
Women
in the Bible*

Intimate portraits of
WOMEN IN THE
BIBLE

Lee Roddy

CHRISTIAN HERALD BOOKS
Chappaqua, New York

220.92
Rod

We acknowledge with appreciation permission to quote from:

The New American Standard Bible, © The Lockman Foundation, 1960, 1962, 1963, 1968, 1971, 1972, 1973, 1975.

JOSEPHUS: *Complete Works of Flavius Josephus*. Kregel Publications, Grand Rapids, Mich., 1974. Used by permission.

Library of Congress Cataloging in Publication Data

Roddy, Lee, 1921—
  Women in the Bible.

Bibliography: p.
  1. Women in the Bible. 2. Bible — Biography.
I. Title.
BS575.R63   220.9′2   [B]   80-65432
ISBN 0-915684-64-0

First Edition
CHRISTIAN HERALD BOOKS, 40 Overlook Drive, Chappaqua, New York 10514
Printed in the United States of America

MEMBER OF
EVANGELICAL CHRISTIAN
PUBLISHERS ASSOCIATION

Christian Herald, independent, evangelical and interdenominational, is dedicated to publishing wholesome, inspirational and religious books for Christian families. "The books you can trust."

4013

To My Six Sisters:
Dee Parker
Vi Greene
Helen Olson
Mary Ann Sellman
Belle Roddy
Lela Daily

Intimate Portraits of the Women in the Bible

Women of the New Testament

8   Preface
9   Anna
11   Bernice
14   Dorcas/Tabitha
18   Drusilla
22   Elizabeth
27   Eunice
28   Herodias: Plotted the death of John the Baptist
30   Lois
32   Martha
36   Mary, the mother of Jesus
56   Mary, the mother of John Mark
57   Mary, Lazarus's sister, or Mary of Bethany
62   Mary, mother of James and Joseph
65   Mary Magdalene
70   Rhoda
73   Salome, an ambitious mother

Women of the Old Testament

79   Bathsheba/Bathshua
88   Esther
97   Eve
102   Hagar/Agar
108   Hannah
112   Leah
119   Miriam
123   Naomi
127   Rachel
133   Rebekah/Rebecca
143   Ruth
148   Tamar, who played the harlot
153   Tamar, daughter of King David
158   Vashti

Unnamed Women of the New Testament
Mothers
164   Peter's mother-in-law
164   Jairus's wife
Wives
165   Peter's wife
165   Pilate's wife
Sisters
167   Jesus' sisters
168   Paul's sister
Daughters
169   Philip's daughters
Widows
170   The Nain widow
Sinful Women
171   Adulterous woman
172   Woman of the city
Symbolic Women
174   Woman with leaven
175   The ten virgins
175   Lamb's bride/Jesus' bride

Unnamed Women of the Old Testament
179   Cain's wife
180   Widow whose son was restored to life
181   Potiphar's wife
185   Jewish slave girl
187   Witch of Endor

189   **Bibliography**

191   **General References**

Preface

This book was born of one woman's spoken need. An informal survey of other women disclosed they, too, felt the same need but had not voiced it.

It began shortly after Belle Roddy received Christ in her early forties. She had no Christian background as an evangelical. She read the Bible and other books, but complained, "I don't understand the Bible too well. I don't find what I want in the books I've read about women. What I'd like is to understand how these women's stories relate to me, now, today. What were their emotions? How did they feel? I want to understand these women as human beings, like me. But I can't find out what they were really like."

That sparked my memory. E. Stanley Jones, the late missionary-statesman, had said something about, "If the Lord shows you a need, that's usually His way of inviting you to do something about it."

The nagging idea of Bible women as human beings turned me to researching. In the end, it seemed there was need for a book by an evangelical Christian about Bible women from a new perspective: their human weakness and strengths, their frailties and accomplishments. Some sources treated these scriptural women as plaster saints, far above mortals of today. Other sources judged some scriptural women by today's standards without considering the culture and the times in which those women lived.

Nowhere could I find a source that treated these women as they were: products of their time and culture, with human emotions, feelings and actions. Yet the Scriptures presented these women as real people who were thrust into all kinds of situations from slavery to queens, from small, petty beings to women of great capabilities, and how they reacted.

Some were very good. Magnificent, in fact.

Some were very bad. Some were between these extremes.

Some were not identified in Scripture, but their stories or a mention of them was deemed important enough that God's Holy Spirit guided the Bible writers to include them.

Since all Scripture is given by divine inspiration, and is for our benefit, surely the lessons of these women's lives were put there by God's own purpose!

But, so far as I could determine, no one had written such a book.

So, with trepidation, this work was begun.

It was necessary to consult many authorities, for the job of a nonfiction writer today is essentially that of a good reporter. Read what the scholars have said, research what few ancient chroniclers have recorded about the culture and the period, and seek out the sources which add color and dimension to the tapestry of the Bible itself.

It became a fascinating, challenging, and very rewarding search.

This book is not an exhaustive study, it is only a guide to help others understand the Bible, and to give them knowledge. It is to be read in conjunction with God's Word and never to replace it. In fact, it is the author's prayer that this book will not only enrich readers' lives but prompt and encourage them to dig deeper into the Scriptures to see what new insights God may reveal.

Each character in this volume is referenced so the reader may go directly to the Bible and read the original story.

Each character is examined with the intention of seeing her as a human being who somehow had an encounter that earned her a niche in the most sacred pages on earth.

Those women whose lives are presented in the following pages show how each reacted to an encounter or confrontation with God's children, and sometimes with the Lord Himself. There is a relevance for readers today in those stories, for the women reacted both favorably and unfavorably, as free choice allows.

Finally, this book was written to satisfy the questions of an informal poll among today's women as to what they most wanted to know from their scriptural counterparts.

May God use this volume to bring you to a keener and closer knowledge of Him, and of His Son, whom we serve and love as evangelical Christians under divine commission to complete the work of winning and discipling all people.

Lee Roddy
September, 1980
San Diego, California

WOMEN OF THE NEW TESTAMENT

ANNA
REFERENCES: Luke 2:36-38
SCRIPTURAL SYNOPSIS:

When Mary and Joseph brought the eight-day-old Jesus to the temple at Jerusalem to perform the requirements of the Law, this prophetess approached the family. She gave thanks to God and spoke of Him to those who were looking for Jerusalem's redemption.

COMMENTARY:

Though this woman is mentioned only in Luke's Gospel, she is important for her perception, or discernment.

She was a prophetess, one of the handful so designated in the entire Bible. A prophetess was one who received a message from God and relayed it to the people. It was, therefore, a very responsible position and represented a closeness to God.

Anna was a very old, devout widow. She was the daughter of Phanuel, a descendant of the lost tribe of Asher. The Asherites had been among those absorbed into the mists of history during the Assyrian deportation. Yet somehow this woman's ancient heritage had been kept intact.

She had either been a widow eighty-four years or was eighty-four years old. The Lukean rendition is not precise. The narrative says she was "advanced in years, having lived with a husband seven years after her marriage, and then as a widow to the age of eighty-four" (2:36-37). The important thing is that she had only been married seven years when her husband died, and she had devoted her life to serving God.

9

She prayed and fasted all the time, staying at the temple. The statement that "she never left the temple" has been challenged on the grounds that the holiest building in the Jewish world was not a place of habitation. But Anna certainly spent her waking hours there, listening and hearing the voice of God.

When Anna saw Mary, Joseph, and the infant Jesus that day in Jerusalem, Simeon, the righteous and devout man who had been looking for the "consolation of Israel" (Luke 2:25) had just held Jesus, blessed God, and prophesied. Immediately upon completion of Simeon's words, Anna came up to the family and began giving thanks to God (Luke 2:38).

She continued to speak of Him to all those who were looking for the Messiah to redeem Jerusalem. But Luke narrates her appearance; there are no quotes from Anna.

That's the end of Anna's brief appearance. However, we can learn more from the narrative.

She knew this Child was the Messiah. As a prophetess, she had undoubtedly heard directly from God about Jesus' birth. She had the spiritual discernment to recognize the Messiah in the form of an eight-day-old Infant.

Anna's first words were praise to God. Like Simeon, she had lived to see the day that Jews had spoken about for generations.

But Anna did more. She continued to speak of Him after Mary and Joseph took Jesus on to complete their purposes in the temple. Anna still told others the Messiah had come.

She apparently continued to speak of Him to those who were looking for Jerusalem's redemption.

At the moment, Roman garrisons acted as an army of occupation throughout the Promised Land. The mad despot, King Herod, jealously guarded his throne by mercilessly slaughtering all who might even be suspected of seeking his crown.

Jesus was the Redeemer of the world.

Anna was privileged to be the first to so proclaim the Redeemer, for Simeon hadn't done that. God allowed a very old, very spiritual widow to know and recognize what that Child represented. And Anna was faithful in thanking God and in proclaiming above all others that redemption was present.

Anna's task was undoubtedly a fulfilling one. Her life had been given to God. In her great old age, she was rewarded by being the first woman to tell the world that Jesus had come as Redeemer.

BERNICE
REFERENCES: Acts 24-26, especially 25:13, 23 and 26:30
SCRIPTURAL SYNOPSIS:

Agrippa and Bernice came to Caesarea to see Festus. He told them about a prisoner, Paul the apostle, whom Felix had left in bonds on religious accusations of the Jewish religious leaders. Agrippa agreed to hear Paul. Bernice was present when the apostle argued his case and almost convinced the king to become a Christian. Bernice apparently was a party to the private discussions afterward.

COMMENTARY:

Although her name is only mentioned three times in the New Testament, two secular sources have left records about Bernice. Tacitus, a Roman pagan historian, wrote of Bernice, as did Josephus, the Jewish historian.

She was born about A.D. 28 to Herod Agrippa I, who is called "the king" in Acts 12:1. Bernice was the great-granddaughter of the infamous Herod the king mentioned in Matthew's account. Bernice's younger sister was Drusilla. Both were beautiful, but Bernice was less so than Drusilla. Their brother was Herod Agrippa II. It was Bernice and Agrippa II who heard Paul at Caesarea.

Bernice was a Jewess who was first married at age thirteen to Marcus, son of Tiberius Julius Alexander. Widowed, she next married her uncle, Herod of Chalcis. They had sons, Berniceanus and Hyrancus. When Bernice's second husband died about A.D. 48, Bernice was only about twenty years old. She remained a widow for some time.

She became what is politely known to history as "consort" to her brother, Agrippa II. Whether this was really an incestuous relationship is not known, but the rumors got so bad that something had to be done. She was therefore married a third time when she was thirty-seven.

This husband was Polemo, king of Cicilia (Polemon II in about A.D. 65). This marriage didn't last, although the king had agreed to be circumcised to marry the beautiful Jewess.

Bernice was a woman of strong opinions, even risking her own neck to intercede on behalf of the Jews. Once she was in Jerusalem to perform vows made to God when she acted nobly for her people.

Josephus explains that people making vows in those days drank no wine and shaved their heads for thirty days before offering sacrifices.

During this period, Bernice went barefooted before Gessius Florus, a procurator whose sanity was doubted.[1] She did this after repeatedly sending her horse-and-guards commanders to intercede for her Jewish people. But during the time of her vow, Roman soldiers turned on her. She managed to retreat to the palace for the night.

However, the Jewish historian declares Bernice abandoned her Jewish faith in continuing extramarital episodes.

Among her lovers was the Roman Vespasian and his son, Titus. She was forty-one, Tacitus declares, when her great beauty and youthful appearance helped her become paramour to the general who destroyed Jerusalem and the temple of God in A.D. 70.

After the holy city and temple were destroyed, Bernice and General Titus traveled together to Rome, where he was a hero. There the couple reluctantly parted, apparently for political purposes or from their pressures. Bernice's former lover, Vespasian, had become emperor. When he died, Titus succeeded him. So Bernice was mistress to very successful men, but pagans for whom she had abandoned her Jewish heritage.

This was the woman Luke included in his book of Acts. With her secular history background, it is perhaps easier now to understand the scene between her brother, Herod Agrippa II, and Paul the apostle.

Porcius Festus, whom Emperor Nero had appointed to succeed Antonius Felix as Judea's governor, had set the stage and backgrounded the prisoner's case for the siblings. Paul had been a prisoner a couple of years, a case left over from Felix's time. Felix had been Bernice's brother-in-law because he had been married to Drusilla.

Festus explained to Bernice and her brother that Paul was a prisoner because he and the Jews had argued over a religious point: "about a certain dead man, Jesus, whom Paul asserted to be alive" (25:19).

Paul had appealed to Caesar as was his right under his Roman citizenship. Agrippa II said he would like to hear the prisoner himself.

The next day, Agrippa II came with his sister in great pomp. They were accompanied by prominent citizens and commanders. Agrippa II told Paul he could speak for himself.

The apostle began giving his testimony. Bernice and her brother listened as Paul told how he had lived as a strict Jewish Pharisee, even persecuting the new group of believers in Jesus. Then one day, Paul said, he had encountered the risen Christ on the road to Damascus. Paul, who had earlier been called by the Jewish name of Saul, had been a changed man since then. It was for his faith in Jesus that Paul was now in chains, he said.

Festus cried out that Paul was out of his mind. Nothing is said of what Bernice thought or said, but her brother had obviously been moved.

When Paul asked if Agrippa II (he never really was king like his father, although Acts refers to him as King Agrippa) believed the prophets, he replied: "In a short time you will persuade me to become a Christian!" (26:28).

Almost persuaded! Yet, when Agrippa II went aside with Governor Festus and his sister to privately discuss the matter, they only agreed that Paul had done nothing worthy of death. And, if Paul hadn't appealed to Caesar, he might have gone free.

There is no further mention of being "almost persuaded." There is no further word on Bernice. She had heard the great apostle himself and had chosen to remain unconvinced.

She apparently died in Rome after Jerusalem fell. Her secular records are as silent on that specific point as the Scriptures.

She was a paradox, and therefore very human. She had stood up against soldiers of the mad procurator, Florus. She had shaved her head, walked barefooted in keeping a vow to God, and yet abandoned her Jewish heritage.

Often married, more often involved in illicit sexual liaisons, touched by incestuous scandal, she was antagonistic to her more beautiful sister and yet was so attractive she was paramour to two Romans who became emperors.

However, the Scriptures show her in a cameo role, sitting beside her "almost persuaded" brother and rejecting Paul's presentation of Christ's life-changing power. And so Bernice demonstrates the human trait of hearing the Gospel, rejecting it, and going on to character deterioration and a niche in the scriptural halls of infamy.

1. Josephus, *Wars of the Jews,* translated by William Whiston, p. 485.

DORCAS/TABITHA
REFERENCE: Acts 9:36-43
SCRIPTURAL SYNOPSIS:

Tabitha, called Dorcas, was a Christian disciple living at Joppa, near Lydda, who did good deeds and gave alms. She became sick and died. The women prepared her body for burial but sent for Peter, who came to the dead woman's chamber. The widows showed items Dorcas had made, but Peter put them out of the room, prayed, and the dead woman rose to life again. The event became widely known, and many people believed in the Lord.

COMMENTARY:

There is a fascinating word in the first sentence of Dorcas's story: "Now there was at Joppa a certain disciple named Tabitha." For the first and only time in the New Testament, the Greek word for "disciple" is used in connection with a woman.

Other disciples are mentioned in the same paragraph without specifying gender, but since the single New Testament use of the Greek word for "disciple" is specifically given to Tabitha, it may logically be assumed the other disciples were men.

Since the Scriptures were inspired of God and written by men under the guidance of the Holy Spirit, we must stop and reflect on this exclusive use of "disciple" for a woman.

We can presume it was no accident. There are many women in the New Testament, including such faithful followers of Jesus as Mary Magdalene, who stood by the cross, saw the tomb sealed, and was the first person spoken to by the risen Savior.

Why single out Tabitha/Dorcas for this exclusive term? It

apparently had to do with her specific activities in Joppa. This was the seacoast town from which Jonah had once sailed. Many widows and orphans were created when men embarked from Joppa for a perilous journey on the "Great Sea," as the Mediterranean was then known. Shipwrecks and storms were frequent conversation topics at Dorcas's hometown.

Here we begin to find a possible hint at Dorcas's title of disciple. She saw a need in those unfortunate people. Many others in Joppa also knew there was a need. Yet Dorcas did something about it. The Scriptures declare she made robes and other items of clothing in acts of charity which made her beloved among the people. She was also credited with "deeds of kindness and charity" on a continual basis (Acts 9:36).

Some translations include "almsgiving" among her good deeds. This English word translated from the Greek means "benovolent giving." One translation uses "acts for charity" for the term which is peculiar to the New Testament. Jesus approved it, providing it was done without fanfare and with a proper spiritual motive.

Here, then, seems to be a solid clue to this remarkable woman called Dorcas today, although her original Aramaic name was Tabitha.

She was a follower of Jesus who put her faith into action with what she had at hand: sewing equipment and some money.

It is assumed Dorcas had some money, but it's not known if she was rich. The text omits such a reference, leaving the implication that she was not wealthy. However, she had a two-story house, which was not uncommon for the times for those who were not poor.

Dorcas was a doer. She gave alms and sewed clothing. These garments were either sold and the money passed on to the needy, or the clothes were sewed and given away. The world needs such women. Yet Dorcas sickened and died, apparently suffering only a short illness.

The women performed the traditional services for the dead, washing Dorcas's body and "laying it out," to use a more modern term, in an upstairs room.

The survivors apparently felt that such a good woman should

not have died. Otherwise, why would they have sent two men to Peter, who was known to be at nearby Lydda? This is a town in the Plain of Sharon, about ten miles southeast of Joppa, but more inland.

Peter had been visiting the saints in Lydda, where he healed a paralytic, Aeneas. The ministry was now reaching beyond Jerusalem, where the early church had been born. There is no indication of what Peter said or thought when he was called to walk about three hours to see a dead woman.

We wonder if Peter planned to perform a miracle. Perhaps he thought he might be used of God to raise this good woman from the dead. We don't know what, if anything, Peter knew about Dorcas. Yet he came to her deathbed.

The Scriptures give us no clues as to Dorcas's marital state or age, although we can reasonably calculate some possibilities. She was associated with widows, so she logically might have been one of their number. No husband is mentioned, and no children. We can assume anyone who had alms to share might once have had a successful husband, now deceased. Dorcas was a good seamstress, so she probably had known a number of years to develop her skill. Since she made so many garments, it seems likely that she had no children to detract from her occupation of sewing and doing good.

Undoubtedly, Peter was informed of the true facts about the dead woman on the walk from Lydda to Joppa, but God apparently didn't feel it was essential to include them for us.

When Peter arrived, the women took him upstairs to the body. Clearly, Dorcas was dead. They had prepared her body for burial. There was no hurry, although it's hard to understand why they sent for Peter unless they just wanted his comforting presence.

The mourners stood around Peter, weeping and displaying the garments the deceased had made. There is no hint that the mourners asked Peter to perform a miracle and raise the woman from the dead. There is a suggestion of finality in that the women had accepted Dorcas's death.

Peter put them all out of the room. It seems to have been his suggestion or idea that he be left alone. Then he knelt and prayed. After praying, he turned toward the dead woman and spoke. "Tabitha, get up."

Dorcas opened her eyes, saw Peter, and sat up. The apostle took the revived woman by the hand and helped her to her feet. Then he called the believers and widows and presented Dorcas alive to them.

Notice that the account says "believers/saints" (depending on which translation is used) and "widows." Apparently not all who proudly showed off Dorcas's handiwork were believers when Peter arrived. But notice that "this became known all over Joppa, and many believed in the Lord."

Why did a good woman like Dorcas die? Obviously, God used her death to win many believers to Christ. The same is often true today, although the dead do not return to life. There are many accounts of people who become Christians as a direct result of someone's death.

Dorcas's story, included in the book of Acts, led to the formation of Dorcas Societies. These societies still perform good deeds along the lines of their model. But there is still another relevant point we can glean from the narrative about this good woman. It can be phrased in the form of a question.

"What did Dorcas do after Peter raised her from the dead?"

The Scriptures don't say. The very absence of any later details in the Scriptures suggests (1) the Gospel writer has no further feeling of need to write about her later life or (2) the lesson for us today is in the existing portion of Acts.

If Dorcas did anything of merit afterward (as she surely did), it's not mentioned because the lesson is in doing while you're here, alive, now!

We should not wait until later to do those things which Christ told us to do. Don't expect to be active when you're older, have time, or whatever other excuse might be used as some form of delay.

Dorcas sickened and died abruptly, apparently well ahead of what anyone expected. But Dorcas had already done her good deeds, had already put feet to her faith, and had left a legacy of active, proven discipleship. She used what she had, when she had it, where she was, and became the only woman in the New Testament to have the Greek word for "disciple" applied to her.

DRUSILLA
REFERENCE: Acts 24:24
SCRIPTURAL SYNOPSIS:
Paul the apostle was a prisoner for his faith when Felix and his Jewish wife, Drusilla, heard him speak about Jesus Christ. Felix was frightened by the prisoner's talk about self-control and judgment and had Paul returned to prison. Except for the one mention, Drusilla is not recorded in the Scriptures.

COMMENTARY:
This single cameo appearance by the Jewish wife of the governor of Judea has intrigued researchers, who've turned up additional data on her.

Josephus pays tribute to Drusilla, saying she "did indeed exceed all other women in beauty."[1]

She was born in A.D. 38, a few years after Jesus was crucified. She was named for Emperor Caligula's sister, who died unexpectedly at age twenty-two.

Our Drusilla was the youngest daughter of Herod Agrippa I, a friend of the insane Caligula. Drusilla was, therefore, a Herod, a direct descendant of another madman whom Matthew calls "Herod the king." Matthew accuses Drusilla's great-grandfather of murdering Jewish baby boys in an attempt to destroy the promised Messiah when Jesus was born. Josephus says Herod the king killed three of his own sons, his favorite wife, and thousands of relatives and court people in an attempt to secure his throne. Drusilla's father was the son of Aristobulus, one of those sons whom the monster of Jerusalem had slain before the so-called Massacre of the Innocents.

Drusilla had two other sisters, Bernice and Mariamne, plus two brothers, Drusus and Agrippa. Drusus died young. Mariamne is of no importance to us, but we'll meet Bernice and Agrippa, whom we'll call Agrippa II, in the New Testament after Drusilla's brief appearance.

When Drusilla was about sixteen years old (A.D. 53), her brother Agrippa II gave her in marriage to Azizus, king of Emesa. He had agreed to be circumcised as a sign of accepting the Jewish faith at a time when the Christian religion was rapidly gaining converts.

Drusilla had earlier been jilted. She had been promised in marriage to Epiphanes, son of King Antiochus. However, he changed his mind about taking the Jewish faith. So one of the great beauties of that era married Azizus.

But that didn't last long. Aneonius Felix saw the teenage beauty and fell in love with her. Felix had been named procurator of Judea in about A.D. 52 by Emperor Caligula. Historically, Felix was cruel. He was corrupt, hoping to be bribed to release the prisoner Paul.

When Felix decided he wanted the lovely Drusilla, he resorted to trickery. Felix sent a Jewish friend named Simon to Drusilla with instructions to pretend he was a magician. Simon's job was to convince Drusilla to leave king Azizus and marry Felix, a non-Jew.

A clue to Drusilla's human nature is seen in how she arrived at the decision to marry the governor of Judea. She was ill-treated by her older sister, Bernice, who seems to have been somewhat more plain in appearance. Bernice was envious of Drusilla and gave her a hard time. So Drusilla figured out a way to escape her sister's ill-treatment and envy.

Drusilla acted ill. The details aren't given by Josephus, but it worked. She transgressed the laws of her forefathers and married Felix, who was no prize. In about A.D. 60, Drusilla had a chance with her husband to hear one of the greatest Christian testimonies of all time.

By then, Drusilla needed to hear an apostle discuss righteousness, self-control, and the coming judgment. Josephus has shown that Drusilla left her first husband, who had accepted the Jewish faith, to marry a scoundrel outside her faith. Suetonius, a pagan writer of the period, claims Felix was Drusilla's third husband.

This was the situation when Drusilla got an opportunity to hear Paul.

Drusilla is represented as sitting with her husband, Felix, while the outspoken apostle discoursed on the realities of Christian faith.

Felix was frightened. But what about Drusilla? It is at such points that the wish is strong for the Bible writers to have done more than they did. We'd like to know more about the thoughts of this beautiful young woman, now in her prime of life, sitting beside her cruel, corrupt, and frightened spouse. Perhaps Drusilla was also afraid. Perhaps she was like her father, Agrippa I, who had persecuted the infant Christian church, killed James, brother of John and son of Zebedee, and finally, in about A.D. 44, had accepted divine acclamation as a god and been stricken dead by the Lord (Acts 12:1-23).

There is an indication of what Drusilla thought when Paul spoke of judgment. She might have thought of her brother, Agrippa II, seventh and last of the Herod dynasty to rule the Jew's homeland. He was an expert on Jewish customs and could answer hard questions, but he was no follower of this Jesus whom Paul served, any more than Drusilla was.

Drusilla's great beauty was still with her that day when she heard Paul. However, the years were sneaking up fast. Her life had been hard, full of intrigue and suspicion. She probably had little peace of mind. She did not know much of the righteousness or self-control Paul spoke about. Those weren't her kinds of words. Neither was the subject of judgment. We can only wonder what Drusilla's mind suggested to her as she and her husband sat listening to Paul that day.

She had no way of knowing that in two years Felix would be replaced by Porcius Festus, whom the new Roman emperor, Nero, would appoint to be governor of Judea. There was no way Drusilla could know that the Jewish revolt (which her brother opposed) was about to burst upon the land.

In a few years, Nero would recite poetry and blame the Christians while Rome burned. Shortly after that the Jews would ineffectively rise up against the Roman occupation forces. The magnificent Jerusalem temple would be destroyed, as Jesus had prophesied. The city of Jerusalem would be ruined, with only the stone wall left standing — that of Herod's palace — today known as the Western Wall, or Wailing Wall.

There was no way that Drusilla could know that in about eight years from the moment she heard Paul's discussion, the Jews — her people — would be losers in the great final battle for Jerusalem. In a few years more, the Jews would be denied admission to their most sacred city and would not again fully hold Jerusalem for more than 1800 years, until the Six Day War of 1967.

We search vainly for clues as to what was going on in the mind of this Jewish beauty. She had been a king's wife; she was now a governor's spouse, listening to the famed apostle of the new way not yet called Christianity.

We don't know what emotions went through Drusilla as she listened to Paul. But it is quite evident that she either did not accept Paul's viewpoint, or she rejected it. With that, she is done as far as the New Testament is concerned.

It is through Josephus that we get one final reference to Drusilla. In A.D. 79, when she would have been forty-one years old, the son she had borne to Felix was near Mount Vesuvius. His wife was with him. The volcano blew up with a roar which is still a marvel today.

Some sources claim Drusilla died in the eruption. Josephus doesn't say that; neither does he make it clear that Drusilla escaped. But her son and daughter-in-law did perish in the "conflagration of the mountain Vesuvius, in the days of Titus Caesar."[2]

So Drusilla, named only once in the New Testament, but a much-discussed beautiful woman in history, fades from us.

But if we look at her as a human being, with passions, ambition, deceitfulness, and two or three marriages, she piques our curiosity. She escaped the jealousy of a somewhat plainer sister, was jilted by one king, married to another, and fell for the machinations of a pretended magician. Drusilla was a great beauty, a mother, and other things. Yet the Scriptures chose not to tell us any of that, or what she thought or felt.

Instead, we know she was a Jewish wife who sat by her governor-husband's side and heard the Gospel of Jesus Christ. That's all. We don't know the answers to the other questions puzzling us today.

Only one thing matters: Drusilla heard the Gospel from Paul. What she did with that message was her own choice and her own responsibility. In that way, readers today are much like Drusilla, whose name appears only once in the Scriptures.

1. Josephus, *Antiquities of the Jews,* translated by William Whiston, p. 420.
2. Ibid.

ELIZABETH
REFERENCES: Luke 1:5-7, 13, 24-25, 40-45, 56-80
SCRIPTURAL SYNOPSIS:

Elizabeth, wife of an elderly priest, was still childless in her old age. Her husband told her one day that he'd been in the temple when an angel announced they were to have a son. He was to be called John, and he would prepare the way for the Messiah.

Elizabeth did conceive. She was visited by a relative, Mary of Nazareth, who was also to bear a son to be named Jesus.

The boy John was born, named, and Elizabeth's husband prophesied of him. He would be the prophet of the Most High.

The Scriptures have nothing more about Elizabeth. It is her son's story more than hers, and Jesus the Christ's more than her son's.

COMMENTARY:

To be old and childless was one of the greatest tragedies which could befall a woman of two thousand years ago. Soon Elizabeth's life would be over, and she would not have given her husband a son; she would not have given the world a child to carry on the family name.

Yet Elizabeth could trace her own family back thirteen centuries to the time of Moses' brother, Aaron the priest. For Elizabeth's Hebrew name was the equivalent of Aaron's wife's name, Elisheba. But now, it seemed, the heritage of her line was to end, for Elizabeth was old and still barren.

Of course, Elizabeth could comfort herself with the rationalization that this was a bad time to bring a child into the world. At present, Herod the king ruled over Judea under authority of the Roman emperor. Herod was a merciless despot who had killed his favorite wife, Mariamne I, plus two of his sons, Alexander and Aristobulus. And another son by still another of his ten wives was imprisoned, waiting for his father's final order to kill him, too.

Herod had probably come to the throne about the time Elizabeth was a bride. Herod wasn't a Jew by birth, but he knew how to maintain control over the Jews. Herod had slaughtered most of his in-laws, plus several thousand Jewish religious leaders. The older Herod got, the meaner he became.

Part of his concern was that the Jews' long-expected Messiah would come and rule in Judea. For centuries, there had been Jewish prophecies about this Messiah. The Hebrew word meant "anointed." The Greek word was "Christ." Greek was a common language because, before the Romans, the Greek-speaking Macedonians under Alexander the Great had conquered Elizabeth's homeland. Before that, over the centuries the Jews had been under other conquerors or deported to Babylon and Assyria. It had been almost a thousand years since King David had united the monarchy.

Over those centuries of exile, deportation, or military occupation in their own homeland, the Jews' hope for the Messiah had grown. Of course, there had been a brief period of home-rule under the Maccabees, but mostly the centuries had seen them as a subjugated people who longed for the Messiah.

As the wife of a priest and from a priestly line, Elizabeth must have known the Scriptures. She must have known that God had said that not only would He send the Messiah, but also that there would first come a forerunner, someone to prepare the way for the Messiah.

About four hundred fifty years before, Malachi had prophecied about this forerunner:

"Behold, I am going to send you Elijah the prophet before the coming of the great and terrible day of the Lord. And he will restore the hearts of the fathers to their children, and the hearts of the children to their fathers" (Mal. 4:5-6).

Elizabeth knew Elijah the prophet had never died. He had been taken up to heaven in a whirlwind involving horses of fire and a fiery chariot. But how would he return? Malachi hadn't said. Perhaps Elizabeth, like other Jews of the time, wondered about this point.

However, God had warned, "My thoughts are not your thoughts, neither are your ways my ways." God had added that His ways and thoughts are higher than man's (Isa. 55:8-9).

Perhaps Elizabeth was thinking on all these things when her whole life was changed. Since the Scriptures tell us only what happened to her husband in the temple, we may speculate on how Elizabeth received the news for which Jews had waited centuries.

She must have been home late one day when her thoughts were

interrupted by a commotion outside the gate. Her body stiffened in fear as she heard many excited voices, but her husband's was not among them.

She hurried through the house and across the courtyard, remembering Zacharias had gone that day to minister in the temple. He'd been gone an unusually long time, Elizabeth realized as she opened the outer gate.

Her husband stood there, speechless but obviously excited about something. Friends who'd accompanied the old priest home gave Elizabeth the few facts they had.

He'd lost his power of speech, but by signs he had conveyed to the men what had happened. He'd seen a vision. An angel had made an announcement to Zacharias.

Elizabeth was naturally anxious to know more. She supplemented his excited signs by providing a stylus and writing tablet.

Slowly, Elizabeth got the whole story.

Her husband had been chosen by lot to enter the Lord's temple and burn incense. While a multitude of people was in prayer outside, the priest had entered the Holy Place. That was next to the Most Holy Place, with only the twin veils separating the two rooms.

As Zacharias had stood at the right side of the incense altar, an angel of the Lord appeared. The old man had been afraid. But the angel identified himself as Gabriel and assured Zacharias he had nothing to fear.

Impatiently, Elizabeth waited for her husband to complete retelling his experience by stylus and signs. But at last it was out, and Elizabeth had the unbelievable news: They were to have a son!

In their old age, Elizabeth and Zacharias were to have a very special child. He would be great in the Lord's sight. The boy, to be named John, was to be filled with the Holy Spirit while still unborn. He would be like the Nazarites of old, not drinking strong drink or even wine.

But it was the Lord's mission for their yet-unconceived child which must have brought a tremendous emotional response from Elizabeth. Their boy would turn many sons of Israel back to the Lord their God.

John was to go as a forerunner before Him in the spirit and

power of Elijah. This son would prepare his people for their Lord!

Elizabeth's reaction likely was mixed with wonder and awe. To finally be a mother! And of such a son! But what about her husband's muteness? Why was he unable to speak?

The stylus scratched again, and the old priest's hands made gestures. Elizabeth nodded in understanding. Zacharias had challenged the angel. "How shall I know this for certain? For I am an old man, and my wife is advanced in years."

The angel had said that because Zacharias had not believed him, the priest would be mute until the day the prophecy was fulfilled.

Ah! Elizabeth understood! Well, she understood what her husband had conveyed to her, but who could understand how the Lord could make an old woman and an old man produce a special child? Fortunately, it wasn't necessary. The ways of the Lord are past finding out. And nothing was or is impossible with God.

So Elizabeth became pregnant. She chose to remain in seclusion for five months. There's a single line of Scripture to tell what was in her mind. "This is the way the Lord has dealt with me in the days when He looked with favor upon me, to take away my disgrace among men" (Luke 1:25).

Some time later, Elizabeth received a visitor. Her much younger relative, Mary, came to call in the hill country of Judah, where the aged, expectant mother lived.

Elizabeth was glad to see her relative who had traveled all the way from the small town of Nazareth in Galilee, to the north.

When Elizabeth heard her relative's voice in greeting, the baby leaped in the old woman's womb. In that instant, Elizabeth was filled with the Holy Spirit.

She knew! In a loud voice she said to Mary, "Blessed among women are you, and blessed is the fruit of your womb! And how has it happened to me, that the mother of my Lord should come to me? For behold, when the sound of your greeting reached my ears, the baby leaped in my womb for joy. And blessed is she who believed that there would be a fulfillment of what had been spoken to her by the Lord" (Luke 1:42-45).

The two expectant mothers shared their joyous, miraculous stories.

The angel Gabriel had appeared to Mary, a virgin betrothed to

Joseph, a carpenter in Galilee. The Child to be born to Joseph and Mary was the Messiah.

Mary remained with Elizabeth for three months and then returned to her home in Nazareth.

Elizabeth's son was born to the great rejoicing of neighbors and relatives. The Lord had displayed His great mercy to her who had been barren.

On the eighth day, at circumcision time, the friends and neighbors naturally assumed the infant would be named Zacharias, after his father. But when the people said this, Elizabeth spoke with surprising conviction.

"No indeed; but he shall be called John" (Luke 1:60).

They replied, "There is no one among your relatives who is called by that name" (1:61).

It wasn't that John wasn't a good name. It was from the Greek Ioannes, which was from the Hebrew Yohanan, meaning "Jehovah has been gracious." But it wasn't a name borne by any of Elizabeth's or Zacharias's relatives. So the questioners turned from the joyous mother to check with the father. What did he want the baby called?

Zacharias indicated he wanted a tablet. When it was handed over, he took the stylus and wrote, "His name is John" (1:63).

Everyone was astonished, except Elizabeth. She knew God had been gracious in giving her a son. But the new mother had another reason for additional gladness, for the moment the aged priest had written the name the angel had given the boy, Zacharias's speech returned. Elizabeth undoubtedly celebrated with her husband as his first words were praise for God.

Elizabeth's emotions must have surged as she heard the visitors buzzing with excitement, asking themselves, "What then will this child turn out to be? For the hand of the Lord was certainly with him" (1:66).

Elizabeth's husband was filled with the Holy Spirit and prophesied, beginning with the words, "Blessed be the Lord God of Israel." Addressing the baby, the priest added:

"And you, child, will be called the prophet of the Most High; for you will go on before the Lord to prepare His ways; to give to His people the knowledge of salvation by the forgiveness of their sins, because of the tender mercy of our God, with which the sunrise from on high will visit us, to shine upon those who sit in darkness and the shadow of death, to guide our feet into the way of peace'' (1:76-79).

Eventually, the faithfulness of this aged couple was greatly rewarded. Out of this one woman came one of the world's most remarkable men, John the Baptist, the Elijah who paved the way for the Lord Jesus Christ.

Blessed are those women who have yearnings but no child, even in old age. God still has purpose in such lives, as proved by Elizabeth.

EUNICE
REFERENCE: 2 Timothy 1:5
SCRIPTURAL SYNOPSIS:

The faith of this woman is mentioned by Paul the apostle in writing to Timothy, his disciple. Eunice was the mother of this outstanding early Christian disciple.

COMMENTARY:

From his Roman prison, Paul wrote of the ''sincere faith'' that dwelt within Timothy. But this faith had first dwelt in his grand-mother and his mother, Eunice.

This family from Lystra had apparently been contacted by Paul during his first missionary journey. Eunice had seemingly learned about Jesus from her mother, from whom she had also learned the Scriptures. In those days, that meant the Old Testament. Eunice had faithfully passed on to her son what she had learned of both the Scriptures and of Jesus.

Eunice was a Jewess like her mother. However, Eunice had married a Greek (Acts 16:1). The people knew that Timothy's father was a Gentile. It was apparently his influence that had kept Timothy from being circumcised until Paul had this done.

After the family was converted to Christianity, Eunice's son had made such progress spiritually that Paul took him along and taught him more about Jesus.

Nothing much is known about Eunice's husband beyond that

already given. It has been assumed he died when Timothy was young, leaving Eunice a widow. Her son was a teenager when Paul saw him on his second missionary trip through their hometown and was impressed with him.

Eunice presumably was pleased that her son had not only known the Scriptures from childhood, but also that Timothy's faith was so great that Paul took the boy as his own spiritual son.

It was a high honor for Eunice and a testimony to what she had done as a mother in the early days of the Christian movement.

HERODIAS: Plotted the death of John the Baptist

REFERENCES: Matthew 14:1-11; Mark 6:14-28; Luke 3:19

SCRIPTURAL SYNOPSIS:

Herodias had been the wife of Philip, described as brother to Herod the Tetrarch. When she divorced Philip and married Herod the Tetrarch, John the Baptist criticized the official for illegally marrying. Herodias wanted her second husband to execute the baptizer, but Herod was afraid of the people. They considered John a prophet.

Herodias bided her time. At her husband's birthday, she had her daughter dance for the tetrarch. He was so pleased with her performance that he promised before witnesses to give the girl anything she wanted. At her mother's prompting, she asked for and received the head of John the Baptist.

COMMENTARY:

Herodias's brief appearance in the New Testament is augmented by the Jewish historian Josephus. From this near-contemporary of the principals, data are provided that help us understand a very complex situation.

Herodias was a granddaughter of Herod the king (as Matthew calls him), or Herod I, who founded a dynasty that ruled through four generations. Herodias was the daughter of a woman named Bernice and of Aristobulus, one of three sons Herod I had murdered to keep the throne for himself. It was this same Herod I (Herodias's grandfather) whom Matthew records ordered all Jewish male babies killed when Jesus was born in Bethlehem.

Herodias first married her uncle, Philip I, or Herod Philip. She divorced him after a daughter, Salome, was born. Herodias married Herod the Tetrarch, or Herod Antipas, a half-brother to Herodias's ex-husband. Herod the Tetrarch had also divorced his wife in order to marry Herodias.

John the Baptist criticized the tetrarch of Galilee for the action. By Jewish standards, it was incestuous, and it was against the law. A brother could not marry his sister-in-law if she had borne a child. There was also the impropriety of both new spouses having divorced their mates to form this illegal union.

Herod Antipas the tetrarch would have liked to silence John the Baptist's criticism, but people regarded John as a prophet, and Herod Antipas was afraid to harm him. Herodias had a grudge against John and determined to have John's life. She planned to use her own daughter, Salome, to accomplish that.

At a birthday party given for Herod, Herodias's daughter danced before her stepfather and all his court officials and military commanders.

In an apparent drunken act of generosity, the tetrarch offered Herodias's daughter anything she asked; even to half of his kingdom. It wasn't really a kingdom, for he was only ruler over a tetrarchy, or a fourth part of a Roman province; in this case, Galilee. It wasn't really the tetratch's to give, either. He ruled by authority of the emperor in Rome. But his grand promise before witnesses gave Herodias the opportunity she had wanted.

When her daughter came to her to query, "What shall I ask for?" Herodias was ready. "The head of John the Baptist" (Mark 6:24).

The Gospels drop further mention of Herodias after she caused John's death. She was still married to Herod Antipas (whom Jesus called "that fox") when Jesus was brought before him a year or so later. Neither the Scriptures nor Josephus mention Herodias in connection with Jesus' trial before the tetrarch.

However, Josephus gives us the sad ending to Herodias's career. When her brother, Agrippa I ("the King" in Acts and "the Great"

in Josephus), became king, Herodias urged her husband to oppose
Agrippa I before the emperor. Herod the Tetrarch did, failed in his
quest, and was banished to Lyons, a city of Gaul.

When the emperor, the insane Gaius (nicknamed Caligula for
Little Boots) learned that the exiled tetrarch's wife was King
Agrippa's sister, the emperor offered to let Herodias escape the
ban.

But she declined, refusing to "forsake him in his misfortunes."

So history remembers Herodias for her final, valiant gesture,
along with her biblical record of causing the death of John the
Baptist. Whatever else her faults — violation of the Jewish laws,
selfishness, hatred, grudge-holder against the Baptist, and schem-
ing to use her daughter to gain her own ends — Herodias ended
up doing one noble thing.

Though she stuck with her husband in exile, her earlier acts
against John the Baptist generally make Herodias one of the Bible's
infamous women.

LOIS
REFERENCE: 2 Timothy 1:5
SCRIPTURAL SYNOPSIS:

Paul the apostle was a prisoner in Rome when he wrote a single
sentence commending the sincere faith of his disciple Timothy.
That faith, Paul noted, "first dwelt in your grandmother Lois" (2
Tim. 1:5).

COMMENTARY:

Lois was a devout Jewess who had become a Christian some
time before Paul wrote. In turn, she had won her daughter, Eunice,
to the faith. Now Lois's grandson, Timothy, was also a believer.

Researchers believe Lois was probably persuaded that Jesus
was the promised Jewish Messiah on Paul's first missionary journey to Lystra, Lois's home (Acts 14; 16:1).

The importance of the grandmother role in reaching two and
three generations with the Gospel is shown in this brief scriptural
mention. It is the only time in the whole Bible that the word
grandmother is used.

The Old Testament has many references to the grandparents' role, both for good and evil, although the masculine reference is usually employed by the writers of that time and culture.

God had told Moses the people were to keep His commandments, "and you shall teach them diligently to your sons and shall talk of them when you sit in your house and when you walk by the way and when you lie down and when you rise up" (Deut. 6:1-7).

The daughters were obviously intended in this passage, though the reference is specifically to sons. The father was to be the priest in his home. However, in Lois's case, there is no indication she had a husband. She appears to have been a widow. So her faith had been imparted to her daughter, Eunice, and in turn, grandson Timothy had become a believer in Jesus.

But there was a background for that faith in Lois's grandson. Paul had written to Timothy, urging him to "continue in the things you have learned and become convinced of, knowing from whom you have learned them; and that from childhood you have known the sacred writings which are able to give you the wisdom that leads to salvation through faith which is in Christ Jesus" (2 Tim. 3:14-15).

Someone — almost surely Lois or Eunice — had grounded Timothy from childhood in his biblical heritage. He knew the Scriptures.

Proverbs proves that with the masculine reference to good grandparents: "A good man leaves an inheritance to his children's children" (13:22).

However, there's also a scriptural warning of what happens when one generation breaks faith with God and does not keep His commandments or teach them to the children and grandchildren:

"So while these nations feared the Lord, they also served their idols; their children likewise and their grandchildren, as their fathers did, so they do to this day" (2 Kings 17:41).

However, those who pass on their spiritual heritage as a legacy to future generations have the assurance of God that this will benefit all:

"But the lovingkindness of the Lord is from everlasting to everlasting on those who fear Him, and His righteousness to children's children'' (Psalm 103:17).

Lois, apparently filling the role of both grandfather and grand-mother in her home, stands alone in the Scriptures with the title of "grandmother." She was faithful in passing on her faith and her knowledge of the Scriptures. She influenced her own daughter and grandchild for the Kingdom of God through Jesus Christ. And today, nearly two thousand years later, Lois represents both the goals and the possibilities that a grandmother can reach through faithful obedience to God and His Son.

MARTHA
REFERENCES: Luke 10:38-42; John 11:1-45
SCRIPTURAL SYNOPSIS:

Luke first presents Martha after he has told the story of the good Samaritan. As Jesus and His band traveled, they came to a village where a woman named Martha welcomed Him into her home. She had a sister, Mary, who sat and listened to Jesus while Martha did all the hostess preparations. Martha asked Jesus to rebuke her sister for this, but Jesus gently pointed out that Martha was worried over so many things when only a few were really important.

John's Gospel identifies Martha's and Mary's village as Bethany, and their brother was Lazarus. The family was loved by Jesus, so when the brother fell sick, the sisters sent for Jesus. Before He arrived, Lazarus died.

Martha went to meet Jesus and there confessed her faith that He was the Christ and that God would give Jesus anything He asked. Jesus called Lazarus from the tomb, even though Martha warned there would be an odor because Lazarus had been dead four days. Later, Martha served at a supper where Jesus and Lazarus were honored.

COMMENTARY:

Martha's story necessarily involves her sister, Mary, their broth-er, Lazarus, and Jesus. But Martha's personality and her feelings are separate and distinct from her siblings'. Martha was very human in her reactions, but she was also warm, hospitable, and practical.

Luke's Gospel declares that Jesus was welcomed into Martha's home. This suggests that she was the older sibling. It is possible she was a widow. The Scriptures do not say this, but if the property were an inheritance from the siblings' father, it would have been the son's.

Martha took her hostess responsibilities seriously. She was "distracted with all her preparations," but her sister, Mary, sat and listened to Jesus. Martha wasn't the type to serve alone and in silence.

Perhaps a hint of a sharp tongue can be felt in Martha's words to Jesus. "Lord, do You not care that my sister has left me to do all the serving alone? Then tell her to help me" (Luke 10:40).

Notice that Martha did not speak to her sister, but to Jesus. It is probable that Mary was the younger sister, and as such, Martha knew speaking to Mary was useless. The younger sister, like sisters everywhere, would have refused or perhaps said something in front of the guests to embarrass the older sister.

Martha's direct approach to Jesus shows how she appreciated His authority. If Jesus spoke, Mary would not refuse. But Jesus' reply must have surprised Martha. He didn't take her side.

"Martha, Martha, you are worried and bothered about so many things; but only a few things are necessary; really only one, for Mary has chosen the good part, which shall not be taken away from her" (Luke 10:42).

The outspoken Martha learned that serving and hospitality were all well and good, but she was worrying about too many things when only one was really important. The good part could not be taken away; that part was what her sister was getting by sitting at Jesus' feet.

Martha's reaction is not recorded, but she obviously bore no hard feelings toward Jesus for His mild reproof.

For only of these three is it specifically stated in Scripture, "Now Jesus loved Martha, and her sister, and Lazarus" (John 11:5).

Again, Martha is listed first. The brother is last, apparently hinting that he was a younger brother. He was not given the position of prominence that most Jewish families would have given the man in that period. But the important point is that although Jesus taught love as a condition of discipleship, only of these three was it said Jesus loved them.

The evidence that the good relationship continued is seen in John's Gospel. In this case, Mary's name is given before Martha's, with Lazarus's name leading both his sisters'. However, the reason was that Lazarus was sick. The sisters sent word to Jesus. The message did not ask for help, but showed the depth of the relationship and the situation: "Lord, behold, he whom You love is sick" (John 11:3).

At the time, Jesus was not in Judea. Jewish religious leaders were waiting there with intentions of stoning Jesus. Yet His love for the siblings was so strong that He went anyway. He did that knowing that in the two-day delay since receiving the message, Lazarus had died.

But Jesus cared enough to place Himself in jeopardy for His friends. He arrived in the vicinity of Jerusalem after Lazarus had been dead four days.

Martha's energetic personality is seen in the fact that when she received word Jesus was coming, she went to meet Him. But Mary stayed in the house.

Martha gently reproved Jesus in her greeting. "Lord, if You had been here, my brother would not have died" (John 11:21).

However, Martha quickly softened the suggestion of criticism. "Even now I know that whatever You ask of God, God will give you" (John 11:22).

Jesus' reply was brief but emphatic. "Your brother shall rise again" (11:23).

Martha's response confirms her faith in a resurrection of the dead, a belief which some Jews did not accept at that time — notably the Sadduccees.

But Jesus gave Martha a new insight into spiritual matters. He spoke the words which still comfort mourners today. "I am the resurrection and the life; he who believes in Me shall live even if he dies"(11:25).

Did Martha believe this?

"Yes, Lord," she replied. "I have believed that You are the Christ, the Son of God, even He who comes into the world" (John 11:27).

The choice of past-tense words shows this was not a decision

Martha had just made. She had already believed that Jesus was the long-awaited Jewish Messiah.

The Scriptures do not make it clear where Martha was but imply that she went into the house and told her sister that Jesus had arrived. Martha is next seen in Scriptures at the tomb with Mary and some Jewish mourners.

Jesus, having already expressed His love for the deceased, gave an order. "Remove the stone" (John 11:39).

Martha's practical nature made her protest. She stood before the cave and protested, "Lord, by this time there will be a stench; for he has been dead four days."

Jesus asked, "Did I not say to you, if you believe, you will see the glory of God?" (John 11:40).

Martha isn't specifically mentioned, but as the acknowledged authority in the family, she must have been the one who gave the order to remove the stone.

Standing in front of the open tomb, Jesus raised His eyes and prayed. "Father, I thank Thee that Thou heardest Me. And I knew that Thou hearest Me always; but because of the people standing around I said it, that they may believe that thou didst send Me" (John 11:41-42).

Jesus concluded His prayer and with a loud voice called Lazarus to come forth. The man who had been dead four days came out of the tomb, bound with the funeral wrappings. Jesus ordered Lazarus freed from the bindings.

Martha's reaction to seeing her dead brother alive again isn't recorded, but her joy can be imagined.

The final incident involving Martha took place six days before the Passover. Jesus had again come to Bethany as the honored guest of Martha, Mary, and Lazarus. Lazarus reclined at table with Jesus while Martha served the meal.

This time, Martha served without complaint. Her sister anointed Jesus' feet, and Judas Iscariot complained about her wasting the costly ointment. Jesus rebuked Judas, an act some researchers believe was the final event which caused Judas to betray the Lord.

Nothing more is said of Martha. In less than a week, Jesus was crucified. But three days later, He had proved the words spoken to Martha: "I am the resurrection...."

So Martha has come down through the centuries as a woman who opened her home to Jesus, who at one point complained to Jesus about her sister, and who later served Jesus with gratitude for what He had done. Martha was very human. She spoke her mind, displayed some sisterly rivalry toward Mary, and yet had such trust in Jesus that her ringing declaration of faith is still with us.

Martha had once been so busy doing things that she had to be gently reproved by Jesus. Though He did not condemn her, He told her that she had lost her peace of mind because she emphasized the wrong things. From Martha we learn that sometimes even the important things, like good hospitality, should take second place to being with Jesus, for that's the best thing in life.

MARY, the mother of Jesus
REFERENCES: Matthew 1:18-25; 2:11-23; 13:55; Mark 3:31; 6:3; Luke 1:26-56; 2:5-19, 22-51; 8:19-21; John 2:1-12; 19:25-27; Acts 1:14
SCRIPTURAL SYNOPSIS:

Mary was a virgin living in the Galilean city of Nazareth when the angel Gabriel told her she would bear a child of the Holy Ghost. The son was to be called Jesus. Mary accepted this angelic announcement, and it came to pass after she visited her relative Elizabeth.

Mary had gone with her husband, Joseph, to the little town of Bethlehem in Judea to be registered in a Roman census. It was in Bethlehem that the Child was born. Both wise men and shepherds came to see the Child, although apparently at different times. The shepherds came when the babe was in the manger where He had been born. The wise men brought gifts to the baby in a house.

Mary and Joseph took the Child to Jerusalem on the eighth day after birth for circumcision and to present the Child to the Lord, as required of first-born Jews.

Mary fled with her husband and the child to Egypt when Herod the king began a massacre of male Jewish babies under age two.

When Herod was dead, Mary and the family returned to their homeland, settling at Nazareth in Galilee.

Each year, Mary went with her husband at Passover to Jerusalem, taking Jesus with them when he was twelve. Mary and Joseph had some anxious days on the return trip when they discovered the boy was missing. They returned to Jerusalem and found Jesus talking to the learned men. Mary rebuked Jesus, but He replied that He had to be about His Father's business.

The family returned to Nazareth, where Jesus was subject to Mary and Joseph, and Mary pondered in her heart all the things she'd seen and heard about her Son.

Mary bore other sons and daughters. Some of the people questioned Jesus' actions when He began His ministry, remembering He was Mary's Son, and that his brothers and sisters lived in the area.

Mary and some of her sons tried to reach Jesus one time during the height of His ministry, causing Jesus to comment allegorically on who His mother and brothers were: namely, those who obeyed God.

Mary's husband is omitted from later references in the Scriptures, leading to speculation that Joseph died and left Mary a widow.

She was at the cross when Jesus was crucified. In one of His last acts, Jesus gave Mary into the keeping of the disciple John. John took Mary into his own home and apparently treated her as his mother.

The Scriptures are silent on Mary's activities after that, except for one brief mention following the resurrection. She and some of her other sons were among those in the upper room after the ascension when Peter gave his first sermon explaining all that had gone before, including the Messianic tie-in with the Old Testament.

There is no further mention of Mary in the New Testament.

COMMENTARY:

Mary, the mother of Jesus, is undoubtedly the most significant woman of the New Testament. She has become so popular that a whole system of religious observance has grown up around her.

But the only authority for Mary's life is the Gospels. Those writings show us this remarkable woman as God saw fit to have her recorded in His inspired Word.

However, the Jewish historian Josephus, who lived shortly after Jesus' time, has left a rich heritage of secular information about the times and other people mentioned in the New Testament. From Josephus we know the history and culture which backgrounds the story of Mary found in the Gospels.

Matthew, first-placed of the four Gospels, opens with a long genealogy. It's traced from Abraham through King David to end with "Joseph, the husband of Mary, by whom was born Jesus, who is called Christ" (Matt. 1:16).

Luke, the only other Gospel writer to include a genealogy, begins at Jesus and works backward through David and Abraham to Seth, son of Adam, son of God (Luke 3:23-38). Luke notes Jesus as "being supposedly the son of Joseph." Nowhere is Mary's genealogy mentioned.

Because Mary's pregnancy was by the Holy Spirit, Joseph was not a direct blood ancestor of Jesus. However, Mary was. Yet there is no hesitancy today to include Jesus as the direct descendant of David, Judah, the patriarchs, and back through Shem, Noah's son, to Adam, the first man.

There is no quarrel with the genealogies or their interpretation. There is, however, the continuing question of why Mary's line is not included. It is one of those things that the divinely inspired Gospel writers did not see fit to include.

The chronological order of the scriptural stories suggests we start with Luke, who gives us some background of the history and the times.

Luke is believed to be the only non-Jewish New Testament writer. As a Greek physician, and therefore a Gentile writing to another non-Jew, he carefully documented the historical scene prior to Mary's entry into the story.

"Now it came about in those days that a decree went out from Caesar Augustus" (Luke 2:1).

Caesar Augustus was on the throne as the first emperor of the entire Roman Empire. He ruled from 31 B.C. until A.D. 14. Augustus ordered a census, a Roman preliminary step to taxing the people. That included the land of the Jews, where Mary lived.

Luke, seeking to establish accuracy, declares this census was "first taken while Quirinius was governor of Syria." Publius Sulpicius Quirinius (also called Cyrenius) was consul in Rome by 12 B.C. In A.D. 6 he was sent to Syria as governor to assess taxes after counting the people. At the time, the Roman captive country of Judea and Galilee was governed from Syria to the northeast. But so far, researchers have been unable to place Quirinius as census taker in the time Luke does. There is a clue, however, in Luke's use of "first census." It's possible there was another Jewish census which has not yet been confirmed by historians.

It is especially noteworthy that, after two thousand years, all of Luke's other historical statements have been confirmed. It is logical to expect that someday archaeologists or other researchers will find the the chronicler was also right about the "first census."

Although Matthew doesn't make it clear in his narrative (since the point wasn't crucial to what he had to say), Herod the king had been on the throne in Judea for many years. He had filled the land with Graeco-Roman structures. The magnificent temple in Jerusalem covered thirty-five acres. It was the Jewish center of worship, yet the white, polished, native-stone structure had been built by Herod along the pagan lines of architecture he so admired.

But Herod was equally famous for his violent, suspicious nature and determination that no one would usurp his throne. This applied to his own family. He had killed two sons by his favorite wife, and a third was waiting to die. Thousands of Jews had been executed, and so had many of Herod's in-laws. Their crimes were usually only suspicions by Herod that they sought his throne.

This was the scene when Mary is introduced in the Scriptures. Her people, the Jews, had long been prisoners in their own land. At present, the Roman occupation forces were in command. Before that, there had been a short period of home rule under the Maccabees. They had thrown off the invaders' successors who'd come after the Greek-speaking Macedonian, Alexander the Great. Greek could still be heard spoken in the village, along with Aramaic and some Hebrew.

And, going back still further, there had been deportation and exiling of Hebrews to Assyria and Babylonia. When some of them had returned, they'd had to struggle to find a place among those peoples who had moved into the Promised Land.

But one good thing had come out of all those centuries of exile, invasion, and foreign occupation forces: the Jews' hopes for a Messiah had risen higher and higher. When the Christ (Greek word for the Hebrew *Messiah,* meaning ''anointed'') came, He would deliver God's people and set up a great kingdom.

Mary, like all Jews of her time, must have known that the prophets of old had prophesied repeatedly that this anointed one would come from King David's line, among other things.

So Mary grew up to young womanhood with the knowledge of the Messianic expectation, the knowledge that the Romans occupied her homeland by force of arms, and the knowledge that Herod had filled the country with foreign architecture and wasn't going to yield his crown to anyone — including the expected Jewish Messiah.

Luke, having established the historical background, introduces readers to how John the Baptist was conceived and then turns to Mary. When Elizabeth was six months pregnant with her son, the angel Gabriel went to Mary with an announcement.

''Hail, favored one! The Lord is with you'' (Luke 1:28).

Mary was troubled at this greeting, but the angel assured her and said she'd found favor with God. ''And behold, you shall conceive in your womb, and bear a son, and you shall name him Jesus.

''He will be great, and will be called the Son of the Most High; and the Lord God will give Him the throne of His father David; and He will reign over the house of Jacob forever; and His kingdom will have no end'' (Luke 1:29-33).

Mary asked a logical but extremely delicate question: ''How can this be, since I am a virgin?'' (Luke 1:34).

The angel explained, ''The Holy Spirit will come upon you, and the power of the Most High will overshadow you; and for that reason the holy offspring shall be called the Son of God'' (Luke 1:35).

Gabriel added that Mary's relative, the aged Elizabeth, had conceived, for nothing is impossible with God.

Mary accepted the angelic pronouncement by saying, ''Behold, the bondslave of the Lord; be it done to me according to your word'' (Luke 1:38).

When the angel departed, Luke declares that Mary went to visit Zacharias and Elizabeth in the hill country of Judea.

Matthew's narrative adds some details about Joseph's reactions. The Jewish marriage customs of that time had two steps. Mary and Joseph were engaged, a binding betrothal which required a bill of divorcement to end even though the couple had not slept together. That would come only after the second step in the marriage. But between the first and second steps, Joseph learned his virgin fiancée was pregnant.

Joseph, according to Matthew's Gospel, was a righteous man who didn't want to disgrace Mary, so he wanted to ''put her away secretly'' (Matt 1:19).

An angel appeared to Joseph in a dream and explained he was not to be afraid to take Mary as his wife. She had conceived of the Holy Spirit and would bear a Son who was to be called Jesus. This was fulfillment of the prophetic declaration, ''Behold, the virgin shall be with child, and shall bear a son, and they shall call his name Immanuel, which translates as 'God with us''' (Matt. 1:23).

Matthew explains that Joseph obeyed the angelic visitor, keeping Mary as his wife but not sleeping with her until after the child was born.

We can only surmise how Mary dealt with the problem which led to Joseph's involvement. When she first told him, obviously he didn't accept her explanation of her pregnancy. Luke dismisses the questions Joseph had and follows Mary to Elizabeth's home. Both Gospels ignore Mary's emotions and thoughts in this sensitive area of culture. But we wonder what Mary thought.

She told her betrothed what had happened, and he didn't accept the truth until an angel confirmed Mary's explanation. Nothing is said about what the neighbors said, but it was a time when a woman could have been stoned for becoming pregnant out of wedlock. One of Joseph's own ancestors, Judah, had caused the pregnancy of Tamar, and she was almost stoned.

This cultural response may have been partially lessened when

Mary left her hometown of Nazareth and went south to Judea to visit Elizabeth.

This trip also gives us an intimate portrait of feminine reaction to pregnancy in a culture where a childless woman was considered to be unfulfilled.

The old woman and the young one, both stirring with life within their bodies, greeted each other with strongly emotional words.

The older woman declared, "Blessed among women are you, and blessed is the fruit of your womb! And how has it happened to me, that the mother of my Lord should come to me?" (Luke 1:43).

Mary responded with what is called the Magnificat, beginning with, "My soul exalts the Lord, and my spirit has rejoiced in God my Savior. For He has had regard for the humble state of His bondslave; for behold, from this time on all generations will count me blessed" (Matt 1:46-48).

The hymn of praise continued, but there is a curious lack of any mention of the anticipated birth. Mary simply praised God.

After three months she returned to Nazareth in Galilee. The Gospels then pick up the story of Mary and Joseph in the little town of Bethlehem. It was there that her days were fulfilled and her baby was born.

Every Christmas for centuries, Mary's story has been told and retold as Jesus' story. But the questions which present themselves are how Mary felt, what she thought, and how she reacted to the very human emotions which must have assaulted her at that time.

She was a young woman, virginal, in a strange town, far from home, about to give birth to her first child, and there wasn't any room for her in the inn. What would a modern woman in Mary's situation think and feel and say and do?

Would she ask, "If God's truly involved in this, why couldn't He have arranged a decent place for the birth instead of this stable? Are they going to find a midwife in time? We're poor; very poor — why couldn't we have had a little money to tide us through this situation?"

There's no indication Mary felt that way. The Bible simply says, "And she gave birth to her first-born son; and she wrapped

Him in cloths, and laid Him in a manger, because there was no room for them in the inn'' (Luke 2:7).

The rest of the Christmas story is too well-known to dwell on here. In passing, however, some examination is necessary on the question of whether Mary had other children after Jesus was born.

Some people claim Mary remained forever a virgin. However, there is strong scriptural evidence that she bore other children. While some sources claim these children were Jesus' cousins, the Gospels are plain.

Matthew wrote of Mary that Joseph ''kept her a virgin until she gave birth to a Son; and he called His name Jesus'' (Matt. 1:25).

Luke is less specific, but still plain enough: ''And she gave birth to her first-born son'' (Luke 2:7).

Matthew's wording clearly suggests Joseph did not keep his wife virginal after Jesus was born. Luke could have said ''only begotten son'' unless he meant that Jesus was the first-born of other brothers and possibly sisters.

Josephus's secular history has a brief reference to ''the brother of Jesus, who was called Christ, whose name was James,'' who was ordered stoned by Albinus after the death of Festus.[1] Josephus also refers to James as ''the Just.''

We'll return to further scriptural evidence that Mary bore other children later in this study. But now let's consider Mary's life in the chronology of the Gospels and the flight to Egypt.

This flight into Egypt took place after Jesus' circumcision at the age of eight days. It might have been as long as two years since Herod the king killed boys up to that age in an effort to make sure the Jewish Messiah did not succeed to his throne.

Before the flight to Egypt, Mary was obedient to the ancient commands concerning purification after a birth. Mary and Joseph also had time to bring Jesus to Jerusalem to present Him to the Lord, as required in the ancient writings (Luke 2:22-23).

As Mary and Joseph brought the Infant into the temple, they were approached by Simeon. This old, righteous, and devout man spoke prophetically as he held the Infant in his arms.

Both Joseph and Mary were amazed at Simeon's comments about Jesus. But Simeon spoke directly to Mary His mother, declaring, ''Behold this Child is appointed for the fall and rise of many in Israel, and for a sign to be opposed — and a sword will pierce even your own soul — to the end that thoughts from many hearts may be revealed'' (Luke 2:34-35).

These were further thoughts for Mary to ponder in her heart along with those she'd treasured since the shepherds visited the manger (Luke 2:19).

Simeon's comments were apparently followed at once by the approach of Anna. She was an eighty-four-year-old widow and prophetess.

Luke does not quote this woman directly, as with Simeon, but declares she ''began giving thanks to God, and continued to speak of Him to all those who were looking for the redemption of Israel'' (Luke 2:38).

Luke's narrative then declares that Mary, Joseph, and Jesus returned to Galilee after ''they had performed everything according to the Law of the Lord.'' There Jesus grew strong, increased in wisdom, and the grace of God was upon Him (Luke 2:39-40).

There Luke leaves the family until Jesus is twelve. And that's an intriguing emphasis, for Luke, believed to be the Gospel's only Gentile author, had declared in his opening statement that he had ''investigated everything carefully from the beginning'' in order to write an accurate chronology.

We wonder why Luke omitted the flight into Egypt that Matthew covers in his narratives. We wonder what Mary thought in this self-imposed exile with her young child. There is no hint that she complained or wondered why God had allowed her to have a child in a strange town, in a stable, and then have to flee for her child's life.

What makes the Matthew account intriguing is the writer's obvious knowledge about the successor to Herod the king. Josephus gives us details that most readers simply pass over in reading about Joseph, Mary, and Jesus' return from Egypt.

We wonder what Mary thought when her husband announced that an angel had told him to return to ''the land of Israel; for those who sought the child's life are dead'' (Matt. 2:20).

Joseph returned from Egypt to his homeland with Mary and the child. ''But when he heard that Archelaus was reigning over

Judea in place of his father Herod, he was afraid to go there. And being warned by God in a dream, he departed for the regions of Galilee, and came and resided in a city called Nazareth, that what was spoken through the prophets might be fulfilled, 'He shall be called a Nazarene' " (Matt. 2:22-23).

Matthew has no further comment on Mary, Joseph, or Jesus until Jesus is grown. However, Luke brings Mary back for a significant event when her Son was twelve. That year, they took Jesus to Jerusalem for the first time, although "his parents used to go to Jerusalem every year at the Feast of the Passover" (Luke 2:41).

This was required of able-bodied Jews who were to travel each spring (March-April) to commemorate the event under Moses when they had finally been freed from Pharoah's slavery in Egypt. The Hebrews had sprinkled blood on their doorposts. They had eaten a special meal that night when death "passed over" the doors with the blood sprinkled on them, but all the Egyptian first-born of man and cattle had died.

Nothing is said about the first Passover Jesus attended with Mary and Joseph, but on their way home, the parents discovered their Son had stayed behind in Jerusalem without their knowledge. They supposed He was in the caravan with relatives and friends.

We learn something more about Mary's personality and human traits when she and Joseph returned to the capital city and found Jesus after three days.

They were "astonished," Luke says, when they found Jesus in the temple, listening and talking to the teachers. Mary, and not Joseph, admonished Jesus.

"Son, why have You treated us this way? Behold, your father and I have been anxiously looking for you."

Jesus' reply showed He already had a sense of mission. "Why is it that you were looking for Me? Did you not know that I had to be in My Father's house?" (Luke 2:48-49).

Jesus, however, obediently went back to Nazareth with His parents and "continued in subjection" to them while "His mother treasured all these things in her heart" (Luke 2:51).

Luke then drops all mention of Mary for a while.

Matthew brings Mary back momentarily in the early part of Jesus' ministry where He preaches in His hometown. The people were astonished at His wisdom and miraculous powers.

They said, "Is not this the carpenter's son? Is not His mother called Mary, and his brothers, James and Joseph and Simon and Judas? And His sisters, are they not all with us? Where then did this man get all these things?" (Matt. 13:55). Mark uses the Greek, Joses, for Joseph (6:3).

Joseph's occupation is revealed here, about thirty years after Jesus was born. Mary and Joseph have a nice family: four brothers who are named, plus at least two sisters. If they were other than brothers and sisters, it seems logical that would be stated as such. It's true that later the followers of Jesus called each other "brother," meaning in the Lord. However, at this point in the New Testament, that terminology is not used.

We also see Mary at another early point in Jesus' ministry. This experience shows something about Mary's personality. John's Gospel places this event earlier than Jesus' controversial appearance at His hometown.

Jesus had chosen His disciples before He attended a wedding in Cana of Galilee. Mary was there also (John 2:1). When the wine gave out, she told Jesus, "They have no wine."

Why did Mary say that? Obviously, she expected He could do something about it. But how did she know? What did Mary know that the Scriptures don't tell us? She isn't an absolutely confirmed believer in Him, as we shall soon see. Yet she knew something special about Jesus.

He replied, "Woman, what do I have to do with you? My hour has not yet come" (John 2:4).

Why did Jesus call her "Woman" instead of Mother? What must Mary have thought of a son who didn't use the more familiar equivalent of Mother? Any woman could have been addressed this way. We don't know the answers, but the term Jesus used, in our culture, doesn't make Him seem warm and likable. In fact, as we'll see later, Jesus' attitude toward His mother and siblings is one of distance. It is not until the final agony of the cross that Jesus' compassion is demonstrated toward His mother.

At the Cana wedding feast, Jesus' comment about His hour not yet being there didn't phase Mary. She said to the servants, "Whatever He says to you, do it" (2:5).

The miracle of turning water into wine was the "beginning of His signs," John's Gospel asserts. His disciples believed in Him. But we're left with a puzzle about what Mary believed of Jesus at that point.

John's Gospel immediately says Jesus went down to Capernaum, "He and His mother, and His brothers, and His disciples" (2:12).

It has been speculated that Joseph was dead, yet the apparently-later episode at Nazareth indicates the carpenter was still living. However, other references strongly suggest that Mary was widowed during the early days of Jesus' ministry. Joseph is omitted, pointedly it seems, from later references to Mary.

Something more of Mary's human traits is revealed in a scriptural episode when Jesus' ministry was flourishing. Multitudes were following Jesus. He was performing miracles, preaching and teaching. In fact, so many people crowded about that when "He came home," Jesus "could not even eat a meal" (Mark 3:21).

The next verse doesn't specifically mention Mary, but she is mentioned shortly thereafter, so she might have been among those whom Mark wrote about. "And when His own people heard of this, they went out to take custody of Him, for they were saying, 'He has lost his senses'" (Mark 3:21). A footnote makes "his own people" into kinsmen, but since we don't know if Joseph had any relatives, and Elizabeth was surely deceased by now, Mary's sister wouldn't have undertaken this alone, so Jesus' siblings seem the most likely to be those Mark meant.

However, unless another change of scene has taken place but isn't made plain, verses which follow shortly thereafter suggest caution in whom Mark meant. Verse 31 declares, "And His mother and His brothers arrived, and standing outside they sent word to Him, and called Him" (3:31).

If Mark 3:21 doesn't mean Jesus' siblings, then we're presented with some enigmatic questions. Who were Jesus' other kinsmen? Why don't the Scriptures tell us? But, if the scene has changed by Mark 3:31, then it can be assumed the same group — His mother and brothers — had earlier approached Him. Or perhaps this second time the boys had brought their mother with them since Mary wasn't with them the first try.

A multitude was sitting around Jesus when someone brought word. "Behold, Your mother and Your brothers are outside looking for You" (Mark 3:32). A footnote declares that later manuscripts also add "and your sisters" to this quotation. Luke 8:19-20 tells essentially the same story about His mother's and brothers' wanting to see Him.

Mark gives Jesus' response to this information as, "Who are My mother and My brothers?' And looking about on those who were sitting around Him, He said, 'Behold, My mother and My brothers! For whoever does the will of God, he is My brother and sister and mother'" (Mark 3:33-35).

What reaction did Mary have when these words were sent back to her? What feelings were aroused in her at such apparent public rebuke?

Since it is known that Jesus' brothers and sisters didn't believe in Him, and they were with Mary, what did they say to her? Brothers and sisters are the same the world over, and their reaction must have stung Mary. Can't you hear their remarks?

"Who does He think He is? We're family! You, Mother, gave Him life in a stable! You fled with Him to Egypt to protect His life! You nursed and fed and cared for Him, and what's the thanks you get? Huh? I'll tell you what thanks He gives you! He publicly refuses to see you or us, his own family!"

Mary must also have suffered from the perhaps-unspoken attitude of doubt from her other children. If they didn't believe in Jesus, as obviously they didn't, then they had to have some doubts about their mother. How did Mary handle that? Had she told them about the angelic announcement of her first-born's conception? Or had she kept her virgin birth experiences to herself, not even sharing them with her daughters?

If we knew the answers, we'd know more about the kind of emotions this tremendously important woman had in her life. We'd understand more how she felt and what she thought in those years when thousands flocked about her first-born, and she was rejected so that Jesus could make a point.

Perhaps there is something we miss in this episode, but on the face of it, Jesus placed strangers above mother and siblings. But in His unique role of God and man in one, perhaps they were not strangers to Him.

Mary's name does not come up again in Scripture until Jesus was dying on the cross of Calvary. While Matthew, Mark, and Luke mention other women at the cross (some by name), Mary, mother of Jesus, is not listed. However, John's Gospel not only shows that Mary, Jesus' mother, was at the cross, but perhaps indicates why the synoptics don't include her among the women.

She may have already gone.

John's account lists Mary right after the early actions of the crucifixion following the incident in which the Roman soldiers cast lots for Jesus' clothing.

"Therefore the soldiers did these things. But there were standing by the cross of Jesus His mother, and His mother's sister, Mary the wife of Clopas, and Mary Magdalene" (John 19:25).

Jesus saw His mother and "the disciple whom He loved" standing near the cross. Jesus said to Mary, "Woman, behold, your son!" (John 19:26).

Even in that hour of excruciating pain from the nails through hands and feet, Jesus addresses His mother by the non-familiar, non-personal "Woman," but His compassion is evident in His next words. For Jesus said to the disciple, John, son of Zebedee, "Behold, your mother!" (John 19:27).

John's Gospel declares, "And from that hour the disciple took her into his own household" (John 19:27).

Could this by why the other Gospel writers don't list Mary, mother of Jesus, at the cross when He dies? Is it possible that John, knowing the end for Jesus was near, obeyed Jesus and immediately (from that hour) led her away from the cross to his home?

That could explain why the synoptics don't mention Mary, Jesus' mother, at the cross: He had known the end was near and had mercifully had her taken away so she could not see his final agony.

Of course, it's bad enough for any mother to see her child executed or murdered or otherwise killed, but it's nice to think

Jesus spared her the final tragic sight of His suffering.

However, there is one discrepancy in this theory: John, son of Zebedee, who wrote the Gospel of John (according to most scholars) was at the cross after Jesus' death. We know this from 19:34, where the soldiers had already broken the legs of the two thieves executed on either side of Jesus (so they would die faster) but didn't break Jesus' legs because He was already dead.

"But one of the soldiers pierced His side with a spear, and immediately there came out blood and water. And he who has seen has borne witness, and his witness is true; and he knows that he is telling the truth, so that you also may believe" (John 19:34-35).

We may logically surmise that John had led Mary away earlier, left her with comforting friends, and then returned to the cross after Jesus was dead.

We cannot imagine Mary's grief from Friday night until Sunday morning unless we have also suffered the loss of a child. However, her pain and anguish and doubts and fears can be visualized.

An angel had appeared to her about thirty-four years before and announced the birth of this Son. Mary had accepted the angel's words without doubt. She had weathered the thoughts Joseph had first had about quietly divorcing her. She had borne Jesus in a strange city, in a manger, and then fled for her life and the life of her Son.

She presented the Child in the temple at Jerusalem as required by ancient law and heard Simeon prophesy about the Infant. "Behold, this Child is appointed for the fall and rise of many in Israel, and for a sign to be opposed — and a sword will pierce even your own soul — to the end that thoughts from many hearts may be revealed" (Luke 2:35).

Did Mary remember those words all those years, and especially on the day her Son died on the cross? Since she treasured other words in her heart, as the Scriptures say, it seems logical she remembered Simeon's prediction.

And what did Anna, the 84-year-old prophetess say to Mary right after Simeon spoke? Luke says only that Anna came up and began giving thanks to God, "and continued to speak of Him to

all those who were looking for the redemption of Jerusalem''
(Luke 2:38).

Did that mean Anna said those things afterward, to other people?
Or did she say something to Joseph and Mary, which Mary
remembered but which the Gospel writer didn't specifically tell
us?

But no matter what she thought that day when her Son died on
the cross, we know it was painful in the extreme, as it would be
for any mother who'd lost a son. It would be more so for the
woman who had known some marvelous and spiritual things we're
not told. Mary knew Jesus had special powers before the wedding
feast at Cana, although we don't know what she knew exactly.

Yet Mary and her sons seemed to have some doubts, for they
had come to save Jesus at a time when they thought He was beside
Himself, or emotionally distressed, in some way.

What were Mary's thoughts when her Son, of whom so much
had been said, died like a criminal when His career had been one
of doing good?

When the sun set to begin the Sabbath, and the tomb was
closed over her first-born's body, what did Mary do? She grieved,
of course. But did she understand what the disciples and other
followers did not — that Jesus would rise again?

What did she think about the ugly rumors that had persisted
among unbelieving Jews and Romans from the very first days of
Jesus' ministry? Those stories were recorded in other non-biblical
literature and persist to this day. Basically, they say Jesus was the
illegitimate son of Mary and a Roman soldier. Surely she must
have heard those stories in her lifetime. How did she feel about
such terrible words? Did these rumors add to her grief so that she
was prostrate the morning after the Sabbath?

Or did wiser heads restrain Mary from joining the other women
who went early to the tomb to finish anointing the body of Jesus?
Think how it would have affected Mary if she had been among
those to whom the angels at the tomb announced the dead was not
dead, but had risen.

And why, we wonder, did Matthew's report of the angel at the
resurrection say, ''Go quickly and tell His disciples that He has

risen from the dead'' instead of saying, ''Go tell Jesus' mother and the disciples. . . . '''?

Mark's narrative is much the same, except that Jesus is said to have first appeared to Mary Magdalene. Although Mary was undoubtedly joyous over the news her Son was risen from the dead, might she have wondered, ''Why couldn't He have first appeared to me and eased my grief sooner?''

Luke lists ''also the other women'' besides Mary Magdalene, Joanna and Mary, mother of James, but quite evidently didn't mean Jesus' mother. John's account is even more restrictive, limited exclusively to Mary Magdalene. It seems plain that Mary, mother of Jesus, was not among the first to know of His resurrection.

The disciples, to whom news of the risen Savior was carried, didn't believe the report. Nothing is said about Jesus' mother and the sensational news. Why? Because the Gospel writers obviously didn't consider that of primary importance.

The news was to the disciples, for they were told what to do, namely, to go to Galilee, where Jesus would go before them. There they'd see Him. The Gospel writers didn't place that amount of importance on Mary's role.

Jesus' post-resurrection appearances were not recorded to include His mother. Jesus appeared to the eleven disciples (Judas Iscariot having committed suicide for betraying his leader) and to two disciples on the road to Emmaus (apparently not the regular eleven disciples, but two others).

The post-resurrection appearances included an incident in Jerusalem where Jesus told the disciples, ''Touch Me,'' and another when Thomas the doubter was invited to put his hands into Jesus' wounds. But nothing is said of Jesus' mother at these appearances.

Did Jesus appear to her privately, we wonder, in an event not recorded? It is hard for us not to see the risen Jesus promptly reassuring and comforting His mother, personally, instead of through words spoken by others, some of whom doubted Jesus had risen from the dead.

But for whatever reason, the Scriptures are silent about Mary from the final words of Jesus to her and John the disciple on the cross until the book of Acts.

Luke is believed to have continued his narrative in Acts. Later, the writings were separated into Luke's Gospel and the book of Acts.

Mary is mentioned for the final time in an offhand, casual way following the ascension. This event is set by Luke in Acts 1:3 after Jesus had repeatedly presented Himself alive "over a period of forty days."

We wonder if Mary was present for this return to heaven. Matthew says nothing of the event, and Mark's record is in the portion omitted in some of the oldest manuscripts. Although John refers to the ascension, no details are given. Luke has a confusing reference to the ascension in 24:51 which seems to suggest Jesus returned to heaven from Bethany the same day as the resurrection; but he obviously didn't mean that, as Acts shows.

In Acts, Jesus gathered "them" together (probably meaning the disciples but allowing room for others) and issued final instructions. We're not told if Mary was there.

Jesus commanded them not to leave Jerusalem but to wait "for what the Father had promised." Jesus referred to the Holy Spirit, with which "you shall be baptized ... not many days from now."

Even at that point, there was confusion in the disciples' minds about what Jesus was going to do. It appears from their recorded question that they did not realize Jesus was going to ascend to His Father.

"Lord, is it at this time You are restoring the kingdom of Israel?"

They seemed to still expect an earthly kingdom for Israel, with the Roman conquerors overthrown and Jesus established as king. Jesus did not correct them but said, in effect, it was none of their business to know God's timetable.

However, "You shall receive power," Jesus promised, "when the Holy Spirit has come upon you; and you shall be My witnesses both in Jerusalem, and in all Judea and Samaria, and even to the remotest part of the earth" (Acts 1:8).

After Jesus said this, "He was lifted up while they were looking on, and a cloud received Him out of their sight'' (Acts 1:9).

Two men in white clothing, obviously angels, gently repri-manded the spectators for standing and looking at the sky. ''This Jesus, who has been taken up from you into heaven, will come in just the same way as you have watched Him go into heaven'' (Acts 1:11).

There is no hint that Jesus' mother was present at this unique event. It didn't seem important for the New Testament writers to record anything about Mary during this most fantastic occurrence.

Instead, she is listed as among those who were gathered in an upper room in Jerusalem after Jesus' ascension. It is noteworthy who's listed ahead of the Lord's mother.

''Peter and John and James and Andrew, Philip and Thomas, Bartholomew and Matthew, James the son of Alphaeus, and Simon the Zealot, and Judas the son of James.

''These all with one mind were continually devoting themselves to prayer, along with the women, and Mary the mother of Jesus, and with His brothers'' (Acts 1:13-14).

Everyone, it seems, has precedence over Mary at this point, except His brothers. Even the women, not otherwise identified, lead Mary and Jesus' brothers in Luke's listing. Peter, as usual, leads the list of apostles, with James and John next. These three were Jesus' closest confidantes during His ministry. It is totally logical that they should head this list, for they had been vital to Jesus' earthly work, and now they were to carry out the Great Commission, empowered by the Holy Spirit.

It is important to notice that something had happened to Jesus' brothers. Before, they had tried to reach Him because they seemed to fear for His emotional or mental well-being. They had been denied admission with their mother in a public event which proba-bly had hurt and stung them. Yet now, after the ascension, they are with their mother and the disciples and the unnamed women, ''all with one mind'' and ''continually devoting themselves to prayer.''

Peter, at this upper room meeting, stands up in the midst of about a hundred and twenty persons, including Mary, and assumes leadership.

Later, when Peter moves on to the Gentiles, James, the Lord's brother, leads the Jerusalem believers. We know from Josephus that Mary then had at least two sons who gave their lives for the new faith: Jesus, then James.

If we ask ourselves seriously about Mary's final appearance in Scripture, several logical answers come to mind.

Mary, like John the Baptist, was to decrease so that Jesus would be magnified. Mary, like many a mother of a well-known Christian, had given birth and early nourishment to someone especially chosen of the Lord. Mary, like other mothers, seems to have been very special in God's eyes to have been entrusted with such a responsibility.

Mary herself had said, "From this time on all generations will count me blessed. For the Mighty One has done great things for me; and holy is His name" (Luke 1:48-49).

She was correct, for she has been counted as blessed during nearly two thousand years. But she was blessed, by her own confession, because God had done great things for her.

She was, like all who hear God's message and obey, blessed because of what God had done for her. She is not special because of who she was, but because of what God did for her. And that's true of the faithful today.

Mary played a vital part in God's plan. She was chosen above all women for this unique ministry of becoming the Lord's mother. But in the end, she was consigned to the position of joining others in prayer.

And that's the lesson of relevance, it seems. God chooses to call some, usually quite unexpectedly as far as the called one is concerned, to have a special mission in life. If that person accepts in faith and obedience, as did Mary, the mother of Jesus, then God does great things, but the glory and the credit belong to Him.

Mary is counted as blessed by all generations, but she gave God the glory, and the Scriptures finally place her in proper perspective when her work is done. She could join the other saints in prayer, but she was not exalted above them. It's hard to remember, but it's a fact from the Scriptures. No matter who we are, the glory belongs only to God.

1. Josephus, *Antiquities of the Jews,* translated by William Whiston, p. 423.

MARY, the mother of John Mark
REFERENCES: Acts 12:12
SCRIPTURAL SYNOPSIS:

The single mention of this woman by name is because of her hospitality. The miraculously free prisoner, Peter, went to the home of Mary, John Mark's mother, where many believers were holding a prayer meeting. Rhoda, a servant girl, responded to Peter's knock. Other verses give some additional insight into this Mary.

COMMENTARY:

Only fragments of facts exist about Mary, mother of John Mark. She had a large home, obviously, for there were "many" gathered to pray for Peter, whom King Agrippa I had imprisoned after killing James, brother of John, with the sword.

The fact that Peter went immediately to this home in Jerusalem after being freed by an angel shows that the disciples were familiar with the place. It has been suggested that the "upper room" where the Last Supper was held was in Mary's home, but this seems to be nothing more than speculation.

Obviously, John Mark's mother was a woman of some substance, not only because of the house's size, but because there were servants. Only Rhoda is mentioned by name, but the fact she's call "a servant" instead of "the servant" suggests there were others.

There is no doubt that Mary, mother of John Mark, hosted what was really the beginning of a church in her home. The interesting aspect there is that she had not sold her home and shared the money in the communal way others had done earlier. For whatever reason, this Mary had continued to own her home.

Since no husband is mentioned, it is possible she was widowed. Her only mentioned child was John Mark, who became one of the church's first missionaries. Since Paul says Mark was Barnabas's cousin (Col. 4:10), Mary was related to the famous traveling companion of the great apostle. It is possible Mary and Barnabas were siblings, which would make Mark a cousin to Barnabas. But that's purely speculation since the Scriptures are unclear on the relationship.

Mary, mother of John Mark, has indicated her human traits by showing us she opened her large home to believers in Jesus Christ. She shared her possession — not by selling it and giving the money — but by making her home a place of fellowship and prayer. The example set by this early Christian mother helped produce one of the first missionaries: her own son.

By keeping what she had but sharing it freely, Mary, mother of John Mark, not only touched her own circle but has reached through two thousand years to touch us by her example.

MARY, Lazarus's sister, or Mary of Bethany
REFERENCES: Luke 10:38-42; John 11:1-45
SCRIPTURAL SYNOPSIS:

Mary is introduced sitting at Jesus' feet while her sister, Martha, does the preparing of hospitality. In exchange with Jesus, Mary's sister learns about priority of values. In the second scriptural incident, Mary has lost her brother, Lazarus, whom Jesus raises to life. In the third and final appearance, Mary breaks a costly jar of ointment and anoints Jesus' feet while He's a guest with Lazarus.
COMMENTARY:

There is some confusion about Mary and an unnamed woman who also broke a bottle of costly ointment to anoint Jesus' feet, but a careful reading of the various accounts shows Mary was only involved in the final anointing just before Jesus' death.

Mary was apparently the younger sister of Martha, into whose home Jesus entered at Bethany outside Jerusalem. The sisters had a brother, Lazarus, believed to have been the youngest sibling. In a society where the son was usually the heir and head of the family, Mary's brother is clearly presented as someone on whom the sisters doted.

Mary's humanness is shown in Luke's introduction of her. She was sitting at the Lord's feet, listening to Jesus, while her sister fussed around with the responsibilities of the home.

Mary must have looked up with some concern when her sister approached Jesus with a complaint. Didn't Jesus care that Mary had left Martha with all the serving? "Then tell her to help me" (Luke 10:40).

Mary, the quiet, attentive one, must have heard their guest gently rebuke Martha. Mary had chosen the good part which could not be taken from her, Jesus explained (Luke 10:42).

Perhaps Mary thought her sister was jealous. Or maybe Mary thought Martha was accusing her of shirking her duty. But Jesus made it plain that Mary was right, while Martha wasn't condemned for having her priorities mixed up.

Mary's emotions are not disclosed in the scriptural account, but it must have been with a sense of satisfaction that she was vindicated by Jesus for choosing to listen to Him over other important — but less important — things.

The distinction between Mary and Martha is further clarified in the second incident recorded about this family. Their brother, Lazarus, was sick. The sisters sent word to Jesus, who was out of the territory because it was not safe for Him to enter Judea. But Lazarus died and was buried in a cave before Jesus reached their area.

When word came to the bereaved sisters that Jesus was coming, Mary stayed in the house while her sister went to meet Jesus.

We naturally wonder why Mary stayed put. It may have been that she was shy, not knowing what to say to the Lord. Her outspoken sister, however, could be depended upon to speak her mind about Jesus' being so slow in coming. Perhaps Mary didn't want to be present when Martha spoke out of her grief to Jesus. Or it may be that Mary was simply always quiet and was a listener more than a talker. In her grief, she might have preferred to stay out of sight, in the home, among friends who mourned with her.

The Scriptures plainly say that Jesus loved Martha, her sister, and Lazarus. There was no distinction, for Jesus loved them all. Although Jesus taught love as a condition of discipleship, it is only of these three siblings that the New Testament says Jesus loved them.

Mary was still in the Bethany house when Martha returned "secretly" with a message. "The Teacher is here, and is calling for you" (John 11:28).

Mary responded by going at once. She met Jesus where Martha had left Him. He had not entered the village, perhaps because His life was in jeopardy and His work was not quite finished.

Mary's leaving the house caused some speculation among the mourners. They assumed she was going to the tomb to weep. Most didn't follow her, although some apparently did. So Mary came alone to Jesus and fell at His feet.

In this moment, we see again the contrast between Mary and Martha.

Mary said exactly the same words her sister had used: ''Lord, if You had been here, my brother would not have died'' (John 11:21).

But what a difference in the attitude of these two sisters! Martha had scolded Jesus, chiding Him for His delay in coming. Mary, on the other hand, fell at His feet and wept.

Jesus, seeing Mary's tears, became deeply moved. He inquired regarding Lazarus, ''Where have you laid him?'' (John 11:34).

Mary got action. When Martha had come to Jesus, He had consoled her with the assurance of eternal life and resurrection for believers in Him, but He had stayed put. Martha had gone back to the village.

The mourners answered Jesus' question about where the body was by saying, ''Lord, come and see'' (John 11:34).

The term *Lord* suggests these Jews had also accepted Him and His message. They didn't ask why Jesus wanted to know where the tomb was; they simply led the way.

The weeping friends and Mary's tears had a distinct effect on Jesus. The shortest verse in the entire Bible sums it up in two terse words of powerful emotional impact: ''Jesus wept'' (John 11:35).

The Jews interpreted that as a sign of how much Jesus loved Lazarus. But some questioned why the One who had opened blind eyes might not have kept Lazarus from dying.

Jesus was deeply moved when He came to the tomb, a cave with a stone covering the entrance. The stone resembled a great millstone on edge. It stood in a shallow trough so it could be moved aside.

Jesus said, ''Remove the stone'' (John 11:39).

Mary said nothing, but her sister did.

''Lord,'' Martha protested, probably in a low, shocked whisper, "By this time there will be a stench; for he has been dead four days" (John 11:39).

The woman who had confessed her great faith a short time ago was now rebuked by the Lord. "Did I not say to you, if you believe, you will see the glory of God?" (John 11:40). The stone was removed.

Mary's emotions can be felt as Jesus began to pray: "Father," Jesus said, raising His eyes, "I thank Thee that Thou heardest Me. And I knew that Thou hearest Me always; but because of the people standing around I said it, that they may believe that Thou didst send Me" (John 11:41-42).

Jesus cried out in a loud voice, "Lazarus, come forth" (John 11:43).

Jesus' voice must have echoed from the open tomb. The effect could have been eerie, causing the mourners to instinctively draw back and huddle closer together. Jesus had raised others from the dead in His brief ministry, but never by calling into a black, echoing tomb for the dead man to come out. Logic dictated that even the most hopeful witness present must have had serious doubts about Jesus; perhaps even Mary experienced that sense of doubt.

The crowd must have stirred uneasily when some faint sounds were heard in the darkened tomb. The people, including Mary, must have involuntarily stepped back and thrown their hands over their mouths to stifle a scream when something moved inside that tomb.

But the Scriptures give only the essential facts: "He who had died came forth, bound hand and foot with wrappings; and his face was wrapped around with a cloth" (11:44).

No doubt the crowd reaction was everything from stunned disbelief to joyousness, with some skeptics pursing their lips in sign of suspected trickery. After all, hadn't Jesus already been accused of sorcery?

It was Jesus' calm voice that many heard above the mixed crowd noises. "Unbind him, and let him go" (11:44).

Simple. Direct. Complete.

The results? "Many therefore of the Jews, who had come to

Mary and beheld what He had done, believed in Him.

"But some of them went away to the Pharisees, and told them the things which Jesus had done" (11:45-46).

The worried religious officials had to take firm action against Jesus. In that moment of joy for the sisters and their again-living brother, final plans were laid to kill Jesus. The religious leaders could not delay any longer.

The story of Mary and her sister and their brother had a sequel. John's Gospel tells how the siblings made a feast for Jesus six days before the Passover. Martha served (naturally), Lazarus reclined at the table with Jesus, and Mary took a pound of ointment and anointed Jesus' feet. She wiped them with her own hair. Judas Iscariot protested. Jesus rebuked him in front of the whole party.

"Let her alone, in order that she may keep it for the day of My burial" (12:7).

If this is the second time Mary anointed Jesus' feet, the Scriptures don't say so. That makes some researchers doubt the accuracy of naming her as the woman who anointed His feet in the home of Simon the leper. It doesn't seem to have been Mary of Bethany.

Judas was ready to betray Jesus. The chief priests were ready to accept Judas's nefarious services. After all, many people who had come to the banquet in Bethany had come not only to see Jesus but to see Lazarus, whom Jesus had raised from the dead. Many Jewish converts were made; they believed in Jesus.

The next day, John's narrative adds, Jesus made His triumphal entry into Jerusalem. The final climactic week of His life had begun.

Of Mary, Martha, and Lazarus, there is no further word. They had served their purpose as far as the four Gospel writers were concerned. After all, this was the story of Jesus. Mary's part had been only a chapter in a greater saga.

And for that, no higher commendation can be given for sisters who disagreed with each other, who behaved completely different from one another, and yet were gracious to the Lord who told us through them, "I am the resurrection and the life."

Mary was the quiet sister, the one who chose to sit and listen at Jesus' feet even though it drew criticism from busy Martha. Anyone can understand the feeling that the house is full of guests and yet one sister is sitting around while the other plays hostess. Yet Mary was right, too, Jesus pointed out.

Mary said the same words to Jesus as her sister, yet she was submissive, not scolding. It seems logical that Mary's words had an entirely different sound from her sister's.

Mary had deep, deep feelings. But rather than talk, she acted out her love by breaking a costly bottle of perfume over the feet of Christ as He reclined beside the brother returned to life.

The lives of Mary and her sister are perhaps best summed up by a modern-day woman who exlaimed, "I love Mary and Martha because sometimes I'm both of them!"

MARY, mother of James and Joseph
REFERENCES: Matthew 27:55-56; 28:1-8; Mark 15:40; 16:1-8; Luke 24:10; John 19:25
SCRIPTURAL SYNOPSIS:

This is one of the six women in the New Testament called Mary. Her appearances are sketchy and brief. She was the mother of James and Joseph/Joses, who had followed Jesus from Galilee. She was among those women who ministered to Jesus in His travels.

This Mary was apparently married to Clopas. She stood at the cross and brought spices to anoint Jesus' body after the Sabbath. She heard the angelic announcement that "He is risen." Her sons became Jesus' disciples.
COMMENTARY:

This Mary is the most controversial of all the six Marys in the Gospels, with scholars over the centuries disagreeing on some aspects of her life.

Careful reading of the Scriptures and comparisons with various researchers' viewpoints suggest the following:

Matthew introduces her as "Mary the mother of James and Joseph" (27:56). She had followed Jesus from Galilee, ministering to Him with others like Mary Magdalene and the wife of Zebedee.

Matthew and John (19:25) place this Mary at the cross. It is John's wording which confuses the issue of exactly who this Mary was. The passage reads, ''But there was standing by the cross of Jesus His mother, and His mother's sister, Mary the wife of Clopas, and Mary Magdalene.''

Three of the six Marys mentioned in the New Testament are present at the cross. The confusion is over Jesus' aunt, who is not mentioned anywhere else in the Scriptures, and whether the identification of Mary the wife of Clopas was meant to be the same as the aunt. It is illogical that two sisters would have been named Mary, yet some students hold to this passage as meaning Mary, mother of Jesus, and Mary, Clopas's wife, were sisters.

The important thing is that the Mary under scrutiny was there at the cross.

The difficulty in sorting out her family also poses problems because of her husband's name. Some sources equate Clopas/Cleophas with Cleopas. The latter was one of the two disciples to whom Jesus showed Himself on the road to Emmaus after the resurrection. But Clopas is an Aramaic name and the other is Greek. While this isn't conclusive, it seems that the two men were not the same; that Clopas's wife was the Mary of this examination.

Therefore, Mary and Clopas had two sons whose identities are also confusing. Matthew calls them James and Joseph (27:56). Luke says ''Mary the mother of James'' (24:10). Mark first calls her ''Mary the mother of James the Less and Joses'' (15:40). A few verses later, the writer identifies her as ''Mary the mother of Joses.'' In both references, Mary is at the cross or at the tomb where Jesus' body was laid.

In the following chapter, verse one, Mark again designates her as ''Mary the mother of James'' and has her at the tomb with spices following the Sabbath.

Luke calls her ''Mary the mother of James'' when referring to her early arrival at the garden tomb and reporting with other women that two men had announced Jesus was risen (Luke 24:10).

Only John has this woman at the cross and identified by her

husband instead of her sons: "Mary the wife of Clopas" (19:25).

The synoptic Gospels (Matthew, Mark, and Luke) place emphasis on this Mary's sons. No mention of her indicates that her sons were Jesus' disciples, but an analysis of the listed disciples shows that this was true.

Matthew's account shows this Mary standing at the cross with the mother of the sons of Zebedee (27:56). We know Zebedee's sons were James and John, two of the closest (with Peter) to the Lord. Yet Matthew calls this Mary's sons James and Joseph. Mark identifies Salome as being at the cross, and researchers have confirmed this was James's and John's mother. Mark lists our Mary's sons as James the Less and Joses (15:40) and then her as the mother of Joses (15:47).

Luke lists our subject only as "the mother of James" (24:10).

Since all four Gospels name a second James (besides the brother of John; Zebedee's sons), it would seemingly be as easy to make this Mary's son, James, as the other one. But Matthew's listing (10:3) confuses the issue by saying, "James the son of Alphaeus." Researchers have concluded that Alphaeus and Clopas are the same.

The consensus is that James the Less (this Mary's son) was the second disciple by that name. Since he was either short of stature of because the James, son of Zebedee, was closer to Jesus, this Mary's son is called James the Less, or James the younger.

Joses is the Greek form of Joseph. There was no disciple by that name. But it is assumed that this Mary was the mother of at least one disciple, James.

The extremely confusing picture of this Mary's relationships is eased by what is said of her in clearer terms.

She was a wife and mother. She followed Jesus with other women from Galilee. This Mary ministered to Jesus and was at the cross, at the near-sunset burial in the garden tomb, and at the sepulcher with spices to be among the first to learn of the resurrection. She apparently had one son among the twelve disciples.

From these facts we can safely assume she was a woman of some means because she could leave her home in Galilee and travel with Jesus, providing with other women for the Lord's needs. This Mary was faithful, staying with Jesus to the cross, seeing where the body was laid, and being up early to complete the burial practice by anointing the body with spices.

Her faithfulness, generosity, and concern were rewarded by being among the first to hear the glad news that Jesus was risen.

So, while details of this Mary's life are uncertain, the human compassion she exhibited makes her one of the few people in the New Testament whose record is unblemished. Her emotions aren't told, but they can be visualized in the various stages through which she passed in following, believing in, and helping proclaim the risen Savior.

MARY MAGDALENE
REFERENCES: Matthew 27:56, 61; 28:1; Mark 15:40, 47; Luke 8:2; 24:10; John 19:25; 20:1, 11, 16, 18.
SCRIPTURAL SYNOPSIS:
Mary Magdalene is mentioned by name fourteen times in the four Gospels, yet very little is known about her except what we can glean from a few brief glimpses. Jesus cast seven devils out of her and she became a faithful follower. She stood at the cross when He was crucified. She was first at the empty tomb and first to report that Jesus had risen from the dead after He personally appeared to her in His resurrected state. Legend says a lot more about her, but that's all the Scriptures say.
COMMENTARY:
In order to draw a proper chronological sketch of Mary Magdalene, we must look first to Luke.

Luke's account tells us that Jesus was going from village to village, proclaiming and preaching the Kingdom of God with the twelve apostles. He adds, "And also some women who had been healed of evil spirits and sicknesses: Mary who was called Magdalene, from whom seven demons had gone out" (Luke 8:2).

That's all Luke says of this fascinating but shadowy woman of intrigue until the resurrection morning.

Matthew's account first mentions Mary Magdalene after the

crucifixion, but refers to her past: ''And many women were there looking on from a distance, who had followed Jesus from Galilee, ministering to Him, among whom was Mary Magdalene'' (Matt. 27:56).

A few verses later, Matthew lists some of those who saw Jesus laid in the tomb. ''And Mary Magdalene was there'' (Matt. 27:61).

Matthew's final reference is in 28:1.''Now after the Sabbath, as it began to dawn toward the first day of the week, Mary Magdalene and the other Mary came to look at the grave.''

Magdalene isn't mentioned by name in the account which follows, but she was obviously present. An earthquake had already occurred. An angel had rolled the stone away. He sat upon it, frightening the guards but reassuring the women.

''Do not be afraid; for I know that you are looking for Jesus who has been crucified. He is not here, for He has risen, just as He said. Come, see the place where He was lying. And go quickly and tell His disciples that He has risen from the dead; and behold, He is going before you into Galilee, there you will see Him; behold, I have told you'' (Matt. 28:5-7).

The women left the tomb quickly ''with fear and great joy'' to report to the disciples. Jesus met the women, Matthew says, and they greeted Him. They clasped His feet and worshiped Him.

Jesus told Mary Magdalene and the other Mary, ''Do not be afraid; go and take word to My brethren to leave for Galilee, and there they shall see Me'' (Matt. 28:10).

While the two Marys were on their way, the tomb guards entered the city and reported to the chief priests the strange events at the garden tomb. The women didn't know, of course, that as they hurried to tell Jesus' disciples of His resurrection, the guards were bribed to say the disciples had stolen the body while they slept.

Luke's second and last reference to Mary Magdalene is in 24:10, where the women have come to the tomb at dawn. The account of two men in dazzling white announcing Jesus' resurrection is much the same as Matthew's narrative, except for the names of the women. Matthew gives only two Marys as being present, but Luke declares, ''Now they were Mary Magdalene and Joanna and Mary the mother of James; also the other women with them were telling these things to the apostles.''

The disciples didn't believe the women's report. Their words "appeared to them as nonsense," Luke declares. And, except for the inclusion of Mary Magdalene in the women who brought the good news, Luke has nothing more to say about her.

Mark's account doesn't mention Mary Magadalene until after the crucifixion and Jesus' death. The temple veil was torn in two. The centurion who had stood near the center cross confessed that Jesus was the Son of God.

Then Mark adds, "And there were some women looking on from afar, among whom were Mary Magdalene, and Mary the mother of James the Less and Joses, and Salome" (Mark 15:40).

Seven verses later, as Jesus is buried and the stone is rolled across the entrance, Mark adds, "And Mary Magdalene and Mary the mother of Joses were looking on to see where He was laid" (Mark 15:47).

In the next chapter, Mark immediately picks up the narrative with verse one. "And when the Sabbath was over, Mary Magdalene, and Mary the mother of James and Salome bought spices, that they might come and anoint Him."

Although Mary Magdalene's name is not specifically given in the next verses, it is clear she was a witness with the other women to the angelic announcement, "He has risen; He is not here" (16:6).

Some of the older Greek manuscripts do not include Mark 16:9-20, but most of our English Bibles do. On that premise, we can count Mark's fourth and final mention of this intriguing woman.

"Now after He had risen early on the first day of the week, He first appeared to Mary Magdalene, from whom He had cast out seven demons" (16:9).

Mark's possibly-spurious ending goes on to tell how Mary Magdalene reported to the mourning, weeping followers that Jesus was alive. They did not believe her.

John's Gospel, coming last in the New Testament's arrangement of those who wrote about Jesus' life, has five specific mentions of Mary Magdalene, more than any other Gospel.

John paves the way for Mary Magdalene by telling how the soldiers gambled for Jesus' clothes. They agreed not to tear the seamless, one-piece woven tunic, or *khiton*, the garment worn next to the skin (19:23-24).

"Therefore the soldiers did these things," John continues, "But there were standing by the cross of Jesus, His mother, and His mother's sister, Mary the wife of Clopas, and Mary Magdalene" (19:25).

John's second reference is in 20:1, "Now on the first day of the week, Mary Magdalene came early to the tomb, while it was still dark, and saw the stone already taken away from the tomb."

She ran to Simon Peter and John with the news. "They have taken away the Lord out of the tomb, and we do not know where they have laid Him" (20:2).

Peter and John ran to the tomb and saw the linen wrappings where Jesus' body had lain. John believed at that point but didn't yet understand the Scriptures. The two disciples returned to their homes.

Mary's first name only is used as John continues his account. "But Mary was standing outside the tomb weeping; and so, as she wept, she stooped and looked into the tomb; and she beheld two angels in white sitting, one at the head, and one at the feet, where the body of Jesus had been lying.

"And they said to her, 'Woman, why are you weeping?'

"She said to them, 'Because they have taken away my Lord, and I do not know where they laid Him'" (20:11-13).

At this point, Mary turned around and saw Jesus but did not recognize Him. He said to her, "Woman, why are you weeping? Whom are you seeking?" (20:15).

Mary, supposing Him to be the gardener, said, "Sir, if you have carried Him away, tell me where you have laid Him, and I will take Him away" (20:15).

Jesus replied, "Mary!" (20:16).

She turned and said to Him in Hebrew, "Rabboni!" which means, "Teacher" (20:16).

Jesus said, "Stop clinging to Me; for I have not yet ascended to the Father; but go to My brethren, and say to them, 'I ascend to

My Father and your Father, and My God and your God' '' (20:17).

Mary Magdalene, John's Gospel adds, ''came, announcing to the disciples, 'I have seen the Lord,' and that He had said these things to her'' (20:18).

The Gospels leave Mary Magdalene's name out from that point on. Neither do the epistles mention her specifically. Mary Magdalene had served the purpose of the Gospel writers, and nothing more needed be said of her for their purposes.

But down through the centuries, this second-most-popular woman of the New Testament has become victim of much apocryphal writing and the target of unfounded legends.

Like many people of her time, she was identified with her hometown, Magdala. This is the Greek word for ''Watchtower.'' Today Mary's town is called Mejdel.

We know that Jesus cast seven demons from her, but there is no hint of where or when this was done. However, Mary became one of Jesus' most faithful followers.

Some sources have tried to equate her with the sinful woman of Luke 7:36-50. It's true the account of the unnamed sinful woman and Mary Magdalene's mention in Luke are relatively close together. But they're not *that* close.

There were no chapters in the original Bible. In the divisions made later, the sinful woman's story was placed at the end of chapter 7, verses 37-50. The first mention of Mary Magdalene is in the early part of the next chapter (8:2), but she is included with other named women. It is illogical to assume she was the sinful woman any more than Susanna, of whom we know nothing. The Lukean account shows a time passage between the sinful woman's washing Jesus' feet with her tears and the introduction of Mary Magdalene.

It seems unfair to have maligned Mary Magdalene, but that's just one of the many legends which have sprung up about this fascinating woman.

Mary's life may be summed up as, ''She was there.''

Once Jesus had cast the seven demons from her, Mary Magdalene followed Him. She was there when the only comfort she could give was to stand by the cross while Jesus suffered and died. She was there when His body was placed in the tomb.

She was there on resurrection morning. Whether she was alone or with other women, Mary was there. And she was there when the risen Christ revealed Himself. Mary Magdalene was there to receive the message and take it to the disciples. Her message was not believed, but Mary had obeyed Jesus and delivered it.

Mary Magdalene was faithful in life, standing when that was all she could do, acting when she could, and demonstrating faithfulness, obedience, and faith in Jesus the Christ. And, just as she was there in Jesus' time, so is her story for us today — a message by example.

RHODA
REFERENCES: Acts 12, especially 12:13
SCRIPTURAL SYNOPSIS:

When Peter was miraculously released from prison, he went to the home of Mary, mother of John Mark, and knocked. The Christians were praying for his release, but when Rhoda answered Peter's knock and ran to tell the prayer meeting group that Peter was outside the gate, they didn't believe her. Finally, Peter was admitted. The people were astonished by his presence.

COMMENTARY:

The concordance lists Rhoda by name only once, in Acts 12:13. However, her story continues through the end of the chapter. The background for her part in the Scriptures is given in the earlier part of the same chapter.

Rhoda must have known, as she went about her work that night, that those were hard times for the infant church.

Rhoda's name translated as ''Rose'' or ''Rosebush,'' depending on whose translation is consulted. Her occupation is even more unclear. One source says she was a slave and that Rhoda was a common name for such people. Other sources call her a ''damsel,'' ''servant girl,'' ''maid,'' and ''maid-servant.''

On the night she got her name in the New Testament, she was at the home of John Mark's mother in Jerusalem. It was a special night for a couple of reasons.

It was the final night of the sacred days of unleavened bread. And it was to be the last night on earth for the disciple Peter, for on the morrow Herod Agrippa I planned to bring Peter forth from prison where he was carefully guarded.

Agrippa I's intentions were clear, as Rhoda must have known that night. The grandson of the infamous Herod the king (Herod I) had begun a persecution of the Jewish followers of the late Jesus, whom some claimed had risen from the dead. Agrippa I had killed the first of the original disciples, James, brother of John and son of Zebedee, by having him run through with the sword.

When Agrippa I saw that this action pleased the Jews, he had Peter, another disciple, seized and carefully guarded. The church earnestly prayed for Peter. The night before Agrippa I planned to bring Peter before the people for trial, Peter was miraculously freed by an angel. Peter headed for the home of John Mark's mother.

Rhoda knew Peter. That is evident from what later happened. We can assume she was a believer and that Peter previously had been to the home where she served.

In those days, a comfortable Jerusalem home might have two stories with a courtyard surrounding the house. Rhoda went to the outer gate but didn't open it. That was sensible, for it was possible that there were more of King Agrippa's men there to seize the prayer band.

Peter called out. Rhoda recognized his voice. And here's where her human traits demonstrated themselves. She was apparently an impulsive girl, for Rhoda was so filled with gladness that she ran inside and announced that Peter was outside the gate.

The poor girl must have been very surprised when those people who had been praying for Peter's release told her bluntly, ''You're out of your mind!'' (Acts 12:15).

Perhaps Rhoda knew from other sources what had happened to Peter. He had been bound with two chains. He slept among four squads (*quaternions*) of four soldiers each; a total of sixteen soldiers. There were guards at the front door of the prison. It was logical that nobody was going to escape from such a tight situation.

Perhaps, because Rhoda was serving while others prayed (and she maybe prayed as she worked), she was the first to know God had answered their petitions.

Peter kept knocking. Rhoda kept insisting that it was really the disciple at the gate. But the prayer band scoffed. ''It is his angel,'' they said (Acts 12:15).

Finally, of course, someone opened the gate and admitted Peter.

Logically, Rhoda should have led the way to the gate. But if she were a slave girl, she might have been ordered to stay behind by those who had prayed, but doubted. Rhoda might have been scolded and her bubbling, joyful nature crushed or subdued by the doubters. We don't know what happened to Rhoda after those in the prayer meeting were unkind to her and suggested that a spiritual angel instead of a living, freed believer stood outside.

We can assume, however, that Rhoda was among those who went to the gate. We can imagine that Rhoda unlocked the gate and threw it wide. We can see her joyful and triumphant look as the people saw Peter in the flesh.

The excitement of Rhoda and the prayer group is hinted at since Peter motioned to them with his hand to be silent. Probably he couldn't make himself heard. He might not have wanted the neighbors to hear, for they might inform any pursuers that there'd been a lot of strange excitement at the home of Mary, John Mark's mother, just around the time Peter had escaped.

We can compare Peter and Rhoda. Several of Peter's earlier experiences with Jesus show the former fisherman was impulsive, just as Rhoda's dashing into the house instead of doing the logical thing by admitting Peter showed her to be. But she was joyous at Peter's voice beyond the gate, so her natural inclination was to run and announce the news.

The prayer group thought she was deluded. But, Rhoda didn't take offense; she just kept insisting. Finally, of course, she was vindicated.

Rhoda was a slave or a servant. She lived about A.D. 43, during the first Christian persecution. She apparently was a domestic in the home of a fairly-well-to-do woman, the mother of John Mark. The home was a center of early worship for those who believed in Jesus Christ, long before they were called Christians.

We learn that this woman of lowly occupation was the first to see that God had answered the prayers of His infant church. Peter was miraculously free to continue his ministry. And only Rhoda, it seems, was able to hear and believe that God had already answered their prayers.

The people prayed, but a servant responded to the evidence of God's answer.

SALOME, an ambitious mother
REFERENCES: Matthew 20:20-24; 27:56; Mark 10:35-41; 15:40-41, 16:1; possibly John 19:25
SCRIPTURAL SYNOPSIS:

The mother of James and John, sons of Zebedee, followed her children and Jesus from the north into Jerusalem. Her sons, with Simon Peter, became Jesus' closest confidantes. Salome asked Jesus to let her sons sit on His right and left hand, respectively, when He came to His kingdom. Salome was also present at the cross and at the tomb on resurrection morning. Salome was the mother of the first martyred disciple, James.

COMMENTARY:

Jesus was ready to go a final time to Jerusalem to face the trials and crucifixion He knew awaited Him there. He took His twelve disciples aside and explained: "Behold, we are going up to Jerusalem; and the Son of Man will be delivered up to the chief priests and scribes, and they will condemn Him to death, and will deliver Him up to the Gentiles to mock and scourge and crucify Him, and on the third day, He will be raised up" (Matt. 20:18-19).

The next verse adds, "Then the mother of the sons of Zebedee came to Him with her sons, bowing down, and making a request of Him."

Jesus asked what she wanted.

She replied, "Command that in Your kingdom those two sons of mine may sit, one on Your right and one on Your left."

Jesus answered, ''You do not know what you are asking for. Are you able to drink the cup that I am about to drink?''

''They said to Him, 'We are able.'

''He said to them, 'My cup you shall drink; but to sit on My right and on My left, this is not Mine to give, but it is for those for whom it has been prepared by My Father.'

''And hearing this, the ten became indignant at the two brothers'' (Matt. 20:20-24).

Mark 10:35-41 tells the same story but omits the mother's participation, saying the brothers, James and John, made the request for themselves.

Judged solely on Matthew's account, this woman comes off as a ''pushy'' mother, ambitious for her sons to be placed above the other ten disciples in the earthly kingdom she apparently expected Jesus to set up in Jerusalem.

Yet this selfish act gives a wrong impression of a woman who cannot be understood without tying together the other references to her.

If we compare Matthew's account of eyewitnesses to the crucifixion with Mark's Gospel, we learn the woman's first name.

''And many women were there looking on from a distance, who had followed Jesus from Galilee, ministering to Him, among whom was Mary Magdalene, along with Mary the mother of James and Joseph, and the mother of the sons of Zebedee'' (Matt. 27:55-56).

Mark's account gives us her name: Salome. ''And there were also some women looking on from afar, among whom were Mary Magdalene, and Mary the mother of James the less and Joses, and Salome'' (Mark 15:40).

This woman who desired that her sons sit on Jesus' right and left hand in His kingdom had followed Jesus from Galilee, ministering with other women to His needs. She stood by at the cross.

In addition, she was one of those who came early to the garden tomb. ''And when the Sabbath was over, Mary Magdalene, and Mary the mother of James, and Salome, bought spices, that they might come and anoint Him. And very early on the first day of the week, they came to the tomb when the sun had risen.

"And they were saying to one another, 'Who will roll away the stone for us from the entrance of the tomb?' "

Mark goes on to say the women found the stone already rolled away. They entered the tomb and saw the "young man" (an angel) who announced, "He has risen" (Mark 16:1-6).

That's the kind of woman Salome really was. It would be unjust to judge her solely on her bold request on behalf of her sons.

We may also see another aspect of Salome in John 19:25. Here we learn that Mary, the mother of Jesus, had an unnamed sister. "But there were standing by the cross of Jesus His mother, and His mother's sister, Mary the wife of Clopas, and Mary Magdalene."

Some Bible students identify Salome, mother of James and John, as Jesus' aunt because of this single reference to the fact Jesus' mother had a sister at the cross. With other accounts of who these women were, Salome becomes a logical possibility. If that were true, then Jesus, James, and John were cousins.

This kinship doesn't seem too farfetched if we look at earlier mentions of the sons of Zebedee. Matthew shows how Jesus began His ministry, calling fishermen brothers Simon Peter and Andrew, and then James and John.

"And going on from there, He saw two other brothers, James the son of Zebedee, and John his brother, in the boat with Zebedee their father, mending their nets; and He called them. And they immediately left the boat and their father, and followed Him" (Matt. 4:21-22).

It has been suggested that Jesus already knew the brothers, James and John. This would be logical if the three were cousins. We know that Zebedee's fishing business must have been hindered by the loss of his two sons, but his wife also gave up some things to follow Jesus.

The family of Zebedee was obvioulsy well-off financially because they had hired servants (Mark 1:20).

James and John were partners with Simon Peter (Luke 5:10) and, by implication, Andrew. While this tie-in with Zebedee reduces somewhat the commonly accepted view that the four fishermen who followed Jesus were poor, the Scriptures make it clear that at least Zebedee and his wife were comfortable.

Traveling with the little band was not an act of a selfish woman. She left her husband to minister to the Lord and His disciples, including her sons.

Salome stayed at the tomb with Jesus' mother and the other women when all they could do was watch and wait. Salome was up early to join the other faithful women at the tomb. She heard the angelic pronouncement, "He is not here; He is risen!"

Later, she became the first mother to know her disciple son had been martyred by the sword. James was the first of the original band to die for his faith.

Salome was undoubtedly dead before her other disciple son, John, late in life, was exiled and wrote the stirring mystical book we call Revelation. But we know that Salome, with her husband and sons, remained loyal to Jesus all their lives. Otherwise, Salome would not have been at the cross and the tomb on resurrection morning.

Salome was a mixture of selfishness and generosity. We can visualize the scene when she gave her sons from the family business to the Lord's business. We can see Salome as she and Zebedee discuss her leaving him with the hired servants and the fishing business to follow her sons and Jesus.

We can imagine her emotions at leaving the security of her home and servants to sleep wherever she could, to eat what came along, to face the dangers of the open road and the hazards of the unknown and unfamiliar.

We can also feel with her the pride that two of her sons were Jesus' closest confidantes, along with Peter. Perhaps we can sense the motives which made her think any family that had given up so much should be honored by having the two sons sit at the right and left hand of Jesus in His kingdom.

We are able to identify with her shortsightedness when Jesus announced He was going to Jerusalem to die, but she didn't understand His real meaning. Salome must have reasoned, if Jesus was the Messiah, as Peter had confessed Him to be and the other followers surely believed, then this Jerusalem trial and death was just another of Jesus' parables.

It seems evident that the disciples and probably all the women who followed Jesus expected Him to leave Jericho, where Salome's plea for her sons occurred, and climb the steep, narrow road up from the warmer city to the mountain capital of Jerusalem, and there be proclaimed Messiah.

So the woman who had left husband, servants, and home to minister to Jesus boldly made a selfish request on hehalf of her sons. She did not ask for herself; she was ambitious for her sons.

We're not told how Salome felt when Jesus turned down her request. Perhaps she thought Jesus' saying the choice of who sat on His right and left hand was a "cop out" so He didn't have to be guilty of refusing her. As a woman reprimanded in front of witnesses, her human nature might have chosen to think so.

The gentle rebuke did not make Salome or her sons quit following Jesus. The Gospels say the other ten disciples were upset with James and John, implying that they understood the mother's motives. They probably liked her, for she had undoubtedly been of comfort and special help along the three years or so of open-road traveling.

The Scriptures don't tell us how Salome felt in that moment, but we know what kind of a woman she was deep inside, and that is what we need to remember.

Salome must not be remembered for her one self-centered request of Jesus, any more than we should be remembered for our own wrongs. Rather, Salome, like all of us, should be remembered for what she was most of the time, a mixture, with the good usually far outweighing an occasional wrong motive or act.

May we remember Salome as we would like to be remembered!

WOMEN OF THE OLD TESTAMENT

BATHSHEBA/BATHSHUA
REFERENCES: 2 Samuel 11:1-27; 12:1-25;
1 Kings 1:31; 2:13, 18-19; 1 Chronicles 3:5
SCRIPTURAL SYNOPSIS:

King David saw Bathsheba bathing and illicitly slept with her although both were already married. Bathsheba became pregnant by David. The king tried unsuccessfully to get her warrior husband home to sleep with her and thereby hide the adulterous nature of the relationship. When Uriah the Hittite, Bathsheba's husband, failed to cooperate, David had him murdered in battle. The child born of David and Bathsheba's adultery died. But David married the now-widowed Bathsheba, who bore Solomon and three other princes.

When King David was dying, Bathsheba helped Solomon gain the throne when one of his half-brothers attempted to seize the crown against David's will. In her later years, Bathsheba was an honored and respected queen mother to whom her son, Solomon, showed special consideration.

COMMENTARY:

Bathsheba faced a difficult situation when she learned King David had sent for her. He had seen her bathing while he walked on the flat palace roof. Bathsheba's beauty prompted him to want to commit adultery with her, though it was an act which was forbidden by God and surely would trigger grave consequences.

Bathsheba was married to Uriah the Hittite, one of David's great warriors. Bathsheba was the daughter of Eliam Ammill,

which translates from the Hebrew as "God is kinsman," suggesting
Bathsheba had a Jewish heritage, although she'd married a Hittite.
Uriah was a hired foreign mercenary whose ancestors (if not he)
worshiped many gods. But Uriah was loyal to David, who had
fought his way up from shepherd boy and fugitive to king of a
solidified monarchy. God had been with David all those difficult
years. A drastic change took place when David sent for Bathsheba.

Bathsheba might have been flattered to have the king send for
her. We don't know if Bathsheba protested when David's desire
was obvious. Under the customs of the time, Bathsheba was
subject to the king's will. But Vashti the Persian queen had stood
up to her husband, the all-powerful king, at the cost of her throne.

There is no scriptural hint of what thoughts tumbled through
Bathsheba's mind when she submitted to David's lust. He already
had wives and children. The beautiful Bathsheba was caught
between loyalty to her husband, who was fighting her king's
enemies in the field while the king stayed in Jerusalem, and the
king's command.

It was a highly risky union for Bathsheba. That danger became
very real when she sent a blunt message to David: "I'm pregnant."

Bathsheba's position was very precarious, but her action suggests she left the matter entirely in David's hands. The king
promptly acted to cover his great sin. He recalled Uriah from
battle and personally ordered the warrior to go to his home.

David was commander-in-chief, but Uriah disobeyed. He slept
outside the king's door instead of sleeping with his wife.

It is likely that Bathsheba knew her husband was close by.
What must she have thought? Should she go to him? Could she
have been such a powerful attraction to a warrior-husband that he
would have overcome his military consecration to keep from women
and slept with his wife? That would have covered David's and
Bathsheba's sin, for the child would then have been legally Uriah's.

David's first failure with Uriah was followed by getting the
soldier drunk. Still, Uriah could not sleep with his wife while his
comrades bivouacked in open fields. Again, it seems likely that
Bathsheba would have known of her husband's drunken condi-

tion. She perhaps could have slipped into the quarters with him. He might have awakened to find her beside him. The coming child's birth could have been covered with legitimacy, yet Bathsheba stayed away from Uriah.

After three days of failure, David ordered Uriah's death. Could Bathsheba have failed to realize that her husband would be murdered because he had not slept with her? David had followed the Lord for years. But now he turned his back on God. He ordered the battlefield murder of a trusted and loyal soldier.

Uriah died in battle by the king's treachery.

Bathsheba mourned for her husband. In those hours and days, she probably reproached herself for adultery. She perhaps considered how she might have saved her husband's life. The Bible is silent on Bathsheba's emotions, but she was human, and her guilty thoughts must have bothered her.

When the mourning was over, David sent for Bathsheba and made her his wife.

As her pregnancy neared its end, David was reproached by Nathan the prophet. David's and Bathsheba's sin was known. God's punishment was coming, but it would hit David harder than Bathsheba. The sword that had struck down Uriah would never depart from David's house. There would be trouble and embarrassment to David's own household from now on. What David did in secret would be known to all his kingdom.

David repented, but it was too late. Nothing is said of Bathsheba's repentance, but she gave birth to a sickly child.

"Then the Lord struck the child that Uriah's widow bore to David" (2 Sam. 12:15).

The king prostrated himself for the child's seven days of life. When the baby died, David ceased his mourning, washed himself, and went to the house of God to worship.

Bathsheba had lost a husband and a child. The anguish must have been great, for what woman could have gone casually through such an experience?

David's and Bathsheba's relationship with God was restored. God promised the king, "Behold a son shall be born to you, who shall be a man of rest; and I will give him rest from all his enemies on every side; for his name shall be Solomon, and I will give peace and quiet to Israel in his days'' (1 Chron. 22:9).

A second son was born to the couple. Nathan the prophet called the boy Jedidah, "for the Lord's sake," because He loved this child. But history calls David's and Bathsheba's son Solomon.

So, out of tragedy, God gave David and Bathsheba the future great king and wisest of all men. Bathsheba also bore David Shimea, Shobab, and Nathan.

However, Bathsheba's problems were not over. When her husband was old and dying, Nathan the prophet's pronouncement of trouble for David's household began to come true. Bathsheba became involved when another of David's sons — Solomon's half-brother — announced he would be king.

At the time Adonijah (son of Haggith and David) drew away some of David's formerly loyal followers. Abishag was caring then for the aged king. Abishag was a beautiful young Shunammite. Bathsheba had become queen mother.

Nathan the prophet, who had brought God's pronouncement of judgment to David years before, now went to Bathsheba with word of the plot.

"Haven't you heard," Nathan said to the queen mother, "that Adonijah has become king, and David doesn't know it? Let me give you advice to save your life and the life of your son, Solomon" (1 Kings 1:11-12).

Bathsheba's own life and that of Solomon rested on the outcome. If Adonijah succeeded in his plans, he would undoubtedly kill both Bathsheba and Solomon.

So Nathan the prophet, now obviously quite elderly, and the no-longer-young Bathsheba, plotted how to tell David the news.

Bathsheba went to the dying king and prostrated herself before him. She realized that death for her and her son was certain if she failed to persuade David to act as she and Nathan wanted.

"What do you wish, Bathsheba?" David asked.

"My lord," the queen mother replied, "you swore to your maidservant by the Lord your God, saying, 'Surely your son Solomon shall be king after me and he shall sit on my throne.' And now, behold, Adonijah is king; and now, my lord the king, you do not know it'' (1 Kings 1:16-18).

Bathsheba explained that Adonijah had sacrificed many sheep, oxen, and fatlings and invited all the king's sons except Solomon. Adonijah was joined by Abiathar the priest and Joab, David's army commander, who had carried out David's long-ago order to have Uriah killed in battle.

Bathsheba concluded her petition by appealing to the king's authority and showing the vulnerability of his son Solomon and herself.

"As for you now, my lord the king, the eyes of all Israel are on you, to tell them who shall sit on the throne of my lord the king after him. Otherwise it will come about, as soon as my lord the king sleeps with his fathers, that I and my son Solomon will be considered offenders'' (1 Kings 1:20-21).

It was delicately put: she and Solomon would be executed if David didn't act promptly and decisively. As Bathsheba finished her remarks, Nathan the prophet arrived as previously agreed. Apparently Bathsheba exited the bedroom while Nathan confirmed her statements, for David listened to the old prophet and then said, "Call Bathsheba to me" (1:28).

The Scriptures don't give us any idea of what she had been thinking. But the fear of death from one of David's other sons undoubtedly weighed heavily on her mind. What if she had failed? What if Nathan the prophet had failed? What if David was too old and weak to act decisively against his son, Adonijah, whom David had never denied anything?

Bathsheba entered the king's bedroom again and stood before him. The Scriptures do not say she bowed and prostrated herself this time. She came at the king's bidding and stood before him. This suggests she was the true queen, ready to face life or death as it presented itself in her husband's next words.

King David opened his remarks with a vow. "As the Lord lives, who has redeemed my life from all distress, surely as I vowed to you by the Lord the God of Israel, saying, 'Your son Solomon shall be king after me, and he shall sit on my throne in my place'; I will indeed do so this day" (1:30).

Bathsheba bowed now, her face to the ground. She prostrated

herself before the king. Her next words suggest the great swirl of feelings which surged through her.

David was dying. They both knew that. But Bathsheba spoke a hope that was not to be, showing her respect for her husband who had just handed her a promise of continued life by keeping an old vow.

"May my lord King David live forever" (1:31).

A few words, but what emotion is suggested in them!

The king issued immediate orders. "Call to me Zadok the priest, Nathan the prophet, and Benaiah the son of Jehoiada" (1:32).

These were several of his long-time followers who had remained true against the desertion of the king's own son, another priest, and the army commander. Zadok and Abiathar had once jointly served as priests. Zadok had once wanted to go with David when another of the king's sons, Absalom, had usurped the power and David had fled from him. Zadok had wanted to take along the Ark of the Lord, but David had sent the priest back to Jerusalem.

Nathan the prophet had brought God's message of trouble to David for his sin with Bathsheba. But that had been a long time ago. David had repented before the Lord and lived righteously since then. Nathan was still loyal to his king.

Benaiah had distinguished himself in battle years ago when David had been a fugitive from Saul's anger. Benaiah had risen to be head of the Cherethite and Pelethites, trusted mercenary body-guards to the king. By now, Benaiah was the third highest ranking commander under David.

Bathsheba knew all this as she stood beside her dying husband's bed that day when he rallied himself to meet the threat from another of his ambitious sons.

When the loyal priest, prophet, and military leader came before David, he ordered them to make preparations for crowning Solomon king.

Bathsheba's part in the anointing of her son is not detailed, but the actions of David's loyal men are in the Bible. We learn that Solomon ascended the throne while his father still lived. Solomon put down the rebellion of his half-brother, Adonijah, and began to consolidate the power of the throne.

Bathsheba reenters the Scriptures for a final dramatic event after her husband, David, is dead and their son Solomon sits on the throne.

Adonijah came to Bathsheba, who greeted him with suspicion. "Do you come peacefully?" she asked (1 Kings 2:13).

"Peacefully," Adonijah replied. Then he added, "I have something to say to you."

Bathsheba's short reply suggests her willingness to listen but hints at some remaining doubts about Adonijah's intentions.

"Speak," Bathsheba said.

Adonijah replied, "You know that the kingdom was mine and that all Israel expected me to be king; however, the kingdom has turned about and become my brother's, for it was his from the Lord. And now I am making one request of you; do not refuse me."

"Speak."

Adonijah said, "Please speak to Solomon the king, for he will not refuse you, that he may give me Abishag the Shunammite as a wife" (1 Kings 2:17).

Bathsheba said, "Very well; I will speak to the king for you" (1 Kings 2:18).

Bathsheba's mind must have seized on the implications of Adonijah's request. It was a second power bid by Adonijah, for whoever had the king's women had challenged the authority of the new ruler. This time, he was not trying to seize the throne so directly. He was more subtle, using the king's own mother to make his plea.

Bathsheba went to her son with Adonijah's words fresh in her mind. Her son's half-brother had said, "You know the kingdom was mine. The people had expected me to be king. But the kingdom went to my brother because God gave it to him." Then the devious thoughts in Adonijah had been voiced without their intent being said.

Did Bathsheba know how her son, now the new king, would see the danger of this subtle threat? Or did Bathsheba simply agree to bring the message from Adonijah to Solomon and let the

king think it through for himself? The Scriptures give no hint, but
we do know that Bathsheba was a wise and cautious woman. She
knew what she was doing, it seems, in approaching her son.

The king rose to meet his mother. Solomon bowed before her,
then sat down on his throne while a throne was brought for
Bathsheba to sit at the king's right hand.

The honor Solomon paid his mother was in sharp contrast to
what had transpired with Bathsheba and David in their final meet-
ings.

Bathsheba said to her son, "I am making one small request of
you; do not refuse me" (1 Kings 2:20).

She had phrased her words well. Her son replied, "Ask, my
mother, for I will not refuse you."

"Let Abishag the Shunammite be given to Adonijah your brother
as a wife."

"And why are you asking Abishag the Shunammite for
Adonijah?" Solomon replied.

The king's next words reflected strong emotion, although the
account in 1 Kings does not reveal what Solomon thought. "Ask
for him also the kingdom — for he is my older brother — even for
him, for Abiathar the priest, and for Joab the son of Zeruiah!"
(2:22).

The Bible isn't at all clear how vital an issue had been broached
by Bathsheba's request for Adonijah, but scholars see great import
in the strong response Solomon made to his mother.

Perhaps Bathsheba understood what was written between the
lines. She was certainly a wise and cautious woman. The years
had dealt more kindly with her than with others of her time. At
David's death, she alone of his wives is given prominence. Her
newly anointed son had honored her by having a throne brought
so she could sit at his right hand. Wise old Nathan had sought her
out to prevent Adonijah's bid for the kingdom before David's
death. So we can assume Bathsheba's thoughts were deep and her
understanding was great in this moment when she asked Solomon
for Abishag as Adonijah's wife, and the king's reply echoed
through the throne room.

It was clear to Solomon that Adonijah was still seeking the

throne. But it is still not easily understood how Solomon viewed the situation. Perhaps Bathsheba understood better than we today.

Solomon was the third king. Saul had been the first. He had been a military dictator who saved the people from their ancient enemy, the Philistines. Saul had relentlessly sought young David's life, but God had preserved the shepherd boy, musician, psalmist, and fugitive. David was chosen by the northern tribes after he had first been made king of the southern peoples. The unified monarchy had given David a chance to begin a dynasty.

The lines of succession were not clearly drawn, for there was no precedent. Solomon was not the oldest son of the late king. David's first-born son, Amnon, had raped his half-sister, Tamar. David's third-born son, Absalom, had avenged his sister by having Amnon killed. Adonijah, David's fourth-born son, had been born in Hebron, before David came to Jerusalem. It was in Jerusalem where he met Bathsheba and sired Solomon. Adonijah's petition for a woman associated with the late King David was clearly a claim to the throne of Solomon.

Solomon knew that and acted, although we can only speculate that Bathsheba must also have known what course of action her son would take.

Solomon had promised his mother he'd give her anything she asked, but he broke his word. He cried, ''May God do so to me and more also, if Adonijah has not spoken this word against his own life. Now therefore as the Lord lives, who has established me on the throne of David my father, and who had made me a house as He promised, surely Adonijah will be put to death today'' (1 Kings 2:23-24).

Solomon acted immediately. Benaiah was sent to kill Adonijah. And, as so often happens when blood is spilled, others died in the backlash, and still more were banished.

Solomon dismissed Abiathar from being priest. Joab was killed as he tried to claim sanctuary by clinging to the horns of the altar. Benaiah became commander of the army. But Solomon's purge did not stop there. He ordered Shimei, who had offended Solomon's father and whom David had allowed to live, to build himself a house and stay in it. If Shimei crossed the Kidron brook outside Jerusalem, he forfeited his pardon and was to die. In time, that happened.

Solomon established the kingdom firmly in his own hands and went on to rule long and well until late in life, when he — the wisest man who ever lived — abandoned his God in favor of his wives' deities and ended up the opposite of his great kingly predecessor.

And Bathsheba? Nothing more is said of her in the Old Testament. We may assume that her son, secure on the throne, treated her well, and that she died as an honored queen mother. Matthew's genealogy of Jesus refers to Bathsheba in connection with David, to whom "was born Solomon by her who had been the wife of Uriah." Bathsheba's name isn't mentioned specifically, but it is clear she was an ancestor of Jesus.

Bathsheba has long been one of the most intriguing women of the Old Testament. Her thoughts are never disclosed in Scriptures, but the gamut of human emotions must have been hers from her position as a valiant soldier's wife to adultery with the king, death, tragedy, intrigue, and murder. And yet, in the end, Bathsheba quietly vanishes into the silence of the centuries except for a brief, indirect reference as an ancestor of Jesus Christ.

ESTHER
REFERENCES: book of Esther
SCRIPTURAL SYNOPSIS:

In the days when King Ahasuerus* ruled over 127 provinces from his capital at Susa, in Persia, the queen was deposed by her husband. In the search for a replacement, a beautiful young virgin, Hadassah, or Esther, was found and taken into the harem. She was obedient to her cousin, Mordecai, and did not reveal her Jewish heritage.

In time, the king's top adviser, Haman, took such a dislike to Mordecai that the adviser decided to have all Jews killed through the king's cooperation.

* Josephus calls this man Cyrus, son of Xerxes. Josephus notes also that the Greeks called Cyrus Artaxerxes, (*Antiquities*, p. 237).

Mordecai sent word to Esther, now the queen, who at first tried to continue hiding her background, then cooperated in a plan to save herself and her people.

Through a series of events, she revealed herself as a Jew but succeeded in having the wicked Haman exposed. In this, Esther was open to great personal harm, even death, but she chose to go with her people.

A day of vengeance was allowed the Jews against those who had planned to kill them and seize their goods. The Jewish festival of Purim began as a result of this story and is still celebrated today.

The story is unique in that it is the only one in the Bible in which there is no reference to God.

COMMENTARY:

Esther isn't introduced until after Queen Vashti has been deposed by her irate husband. Esther is first seen as an orphan being cared for by her cousin, Mordecai, a Benjamite. He is said to have been taken captive in Jerusalem under Nebuchadnezzar, king of Babylon, and deported to Babylonia when Jeconiah was king of Judah.

Some time had elapsed. Esther, or Hadassah (to use her original Hebrew name, meaning ''Myrtle''), was born in captivity in Babylonia.

The Scriptures tell us a lot about Esther. She was very beautiful. She got along well with people, including Hegai, the eunuch in whose charge she was in the days of preparation for first visiting the king. Hegai gave Esther special food and cosmetics plus a separate place in the harem where seven choice maids assisted her.

At Mordecai's command, Esther had kept her Jewish background secret. It is assumed that the maids and the eunuch thought she was a Persian.

Esther also listened to Hegai's instructions on how to deal with the king when she was finally summoned.

Usually, a candidate visited the king once, received gifts, and was placed in a second harem. There she remained until and if the king sent for her again. But Esther, who had heeded good advice all along, was chosen queen; she was the favorite of a man whose authority was absolute.

Josephus says Mordecai was her uncle,[1] but the Scriptures say she was the "daughter of Abihail the uncle of Mordecai" (2:15), which would make Esther and Mordecai cousins. Josephus also says Esther "was the most beautiful" of all the queenly candidates, and "that the grace of her countenance drew the eyes of the spectators principally upon her."[2]

Esther had listened to counsel from her benefactor and the eunuch and ended up as the king's favorite. She had one secret which was ultimately to put her in jeopardy; she hadn't told the king she was Jewish.

The events built slowly to the danger point for the queen and Mordecai.

First, Mordecai learned that two of the king's doorkeepers, chamberlains, and other close officials planned to seize the king. Mordecai got word to Esther, who told the king and thwarted the plot. The two conspirators were hanged, but no reward was given Mordecai.

The next step came when King Ahasuerus promoted Haman, a descendant of the Agagites. This vain, haughty man was delighted when everyone bowed down to him — except Mordecai. Haman decided to punish not only the Jew who wouldn't bow, but all Jews in the various provinces. Haman obtained the king's backing and so planned the genocide of the Jews. In the culture of his time, he cast lots, called Pur, to determine the best day for carrying out his plan.

The Jews got the word of their coming deaths. They mourned, fasted, and wept. Some lay in sackcloth and ashes. Mordecai tore his clothes, donned sackcloth and ashes, and wailed loudly and bitterly.

Esther tried vainly to comfort him. The word came back. For the first time, Esther learned what every other Jew in the provinces knew. Mordecai made the situation official by sending his cousin a copy of the genocide edict.

But Mordecai went further: he asked her to intervene with the king.

. Esther balked. In the custom of the time, it was death for anyone — even the queen — to enter the king's inner court without being summoned. Josephus adds to the scriptural narrative by saying that men with axes in hand stood about the king's throne to punish those who dared approach unbidden.[3]

There was, however, one small possibility of leniency. If the king saw a person approaching unbidden and he held out his golden scepter for that person to touch, that intruder would live.

Obviously, some time had passed (about ten years it seems), and the king's desire for Esther's company had slackened. He hadn't sent for her in a month. She was afraid to take a chance on approaching him unbidden.

Mordecai's reply to his cousin was a warning. She mustn't think she'd escape the Jews' mass execution, not even in the palace. Then he softened the threat with an appeal: how did she know whether or not she had come to the throne for such a time as this?

That got to her. Esther asked her cousin to have all the Jews fast. She and her maids would also fast. After three days and nights, she would take action. Her words show her state of mind:

"I will go to the king, which is not according to the law; and if I perish, I perish" (Esther 4:16). There is no mention of God or prayers, even in this extreme emergency. But Esther and her people depended on fasting, which may imply prayers.

Esther's character development is seen in her change from fear for her own life to willingness to die for her people. She would get involved by revealing her Jewish background. But she wasn't going to just barge into the king's palace, either. She was a smart woman with the courage to risk her life, but only after working out a plan which might prevent her death.

She dressed in her finest royal apparel and stood in the inner court of the king's palace in front of his throne. The king saw her standing there and summoned her. She approached, touched the scepter, and replied to the king's question on what she wanted.

If it pleased the king, Esther would like him to come to a banquet she had prepared. And she'd like Haman to also be a guest.

At the banquet, Esther still remained cautious. She resisted telling her husband what she had in mind. He made it tempting: speak up, and she could have whatever she wanted, even to half of the kingdom. But Esther delayed.

Would the king and Haman come to another banquet tomorrow? Then she would tell the king what she wanted.

Haman was so proud he nearly burst. He was so pleased with his standing in the sight of the king and queen that he didn't even get upset when Mordecai still refused to bow to him.

Esther's reasons for not revealing her thoughts that first night are open to debate. Some researchers feel she got "cold feet" and backed out. Others believe she used the delaying tactics to further build up Haman's already inflated ego.

Haman went to his wife, Zeresh, and friends and bragged about himself. Yet, he admitted, not even this was enough to take away the anger he felt over the Jew, Mordecai, who wouldn't bow to him. So the friends and Haman's wife suggested he build a high gallows on which to hang Mordecai when the time came.

The Scriptures do not disclose Esther's thinking or activities that night and the next. Instead, the narrative shifts to the palace, to a sleepless and restless king. He calls for the official records and "just happens" to be read about the part Mordecai had played in saving Ahasuerus from the late conspirators.

When the king learned nothing had been done to reward the man who'd saved his life, Ahasuerus asked who was in the court. Again, it just so happened that Haman was there. The king summoned him and asked what should be done to honor a man who had pleased the king.

Haman was sure the king meant him and was just playing a game. So the official's ego suggested some impressive public displays. Then the king told Haman that was what he wanted Mordecai to have, and Haman was to bestow the honors!

The infuriated and humiliated Haman had just finished doing public homage to his hated target, Mordecai, when his wife and friends warned him he was in danger. But at that moment the summons came to the second banquet.

There are various possibilities on why it all came together as it did. It may be speculated that God (although omitted from the narrative) had set all the events in place and Esther was wise enough to have sensed this and delayed. From a storyteller's viewpoint, it adds to the suspense. So the true reason for the queen's second banquet will likely never be known.

It was a perfect trap. The unsuspecting Haman sat down proudly with the queen and king. Then, when he couldn't leave, Esther told the king what was on her mind.

She couched her words in careful terms of respect. "If I have favor in your sight, O king, and if it please the king, let my life by given me as my petition, and my people as my request" (Esther 7:3).

What? The queen wanted her life given her? And the lives of her people?

Esther's eyes can be visualized at this moment; downcast in supplication, perhaps moist with the intensity of her feelings. But she didn't wait for the king's questions. She explained that she and her people were to be killed. If they were only being sold as slaves, Esther would have kept quiet because she didn't want to annoy the king. But this trouble was big enough to bring to the king's attention, so she was doing that.

The king demanded to know who had presumed to do this.

Esther's eyes can be seen, lifting, steadying, then plunging, rapier-like, into the hapless guest who sat at the table with her and the king. "A foe and an enemy, is this wicked Haman!" (7:6)

The king angrily stalked out into the palace garden. The Scriptures leave us with the queen and Haman. He begged for his life. He must have impulsively grasped the queen in some sort of impassioned embrace, for the king walked back in and thought the worst.

"Will he even assault the queen with me in the house?" (7:8). Josephus declares Haman fell upon the king's bed. Whatever it was, the king acted.

Haman was seized and hanged on the very gallows he had erected for Mordecai.

A few minutes before, evil had seemed triumphant. Now good and the queen were triumphant. But the story did not end at that point.

A close reading of the Scriptures is necessary to understand what happened next.

Esther again approached the king's throne room unbidden. She fell at his feet. The king extended the golden scepter to her. She arose and stood before the king. Again, she spoke politely and with the subservience required of even a queen of that culture and time.

But her request was plain when she got around to it: let the king revoke the execution order which still stood although Haman was dead.

The king's reply at first seems puzzling, for he reminds Esther he had given Haman's house to Mordecai. The king had even given his signet ring to Mordecai after having it removed from the late Haman's hand. The ring gave Mordecai authority to do as he wished in the king's name — but even the king could not stop action on a decree that had been written in his name and sealed with his ring (8:8). A footnote in Josephus confirms that the "law of the Medes and Persians," properly signed, was irrevocable.

The only alternative left the Jews was to be allowed to arm themselves to resist the coming attack. The king's own prize horses were used to carry the new instructions to Jews all over the kingdom.

The king's latest edict, signed by the signet ring in Mordecai's possession, allowed the Jews to assemble, defend, and then take offensive action against any people or province that attacked them. Not even women and children were to be spared. And the victorious Jews might seize spoils.

The Jews received the news with joy. On the mass execution day Haman had set, when the Jews' enemies attacked, they were repulsed and defeated.

News of the bloody encounter was brought to Esther by the king himself. The Jews had killed five hundred men in the capital alone, including Haman's ten sons. The report from the rest of the provinces wasn't in, but after it was learned some seventy-five thousand had died.

King Ahasuerus wanted to know what Esther desired now. Her answer is surprising. She wanted the Jews in the capital to hang Haman's sons. Her request suggests she wanted their bodies publicly displayed as a warning. It was a gruesome request and casts a pall over the shining example of a young woman acting bravely on behalf of her people.

A time of potential mass murder had been averted, those who planned to kill the Jews were themselves dead, and some of their goods had been seized.

Out of this event came Purim, a celebration still observed by the Jews. It was established by Esther's command in cooperation with her cousin, Mordecai.

The commemoration of Purim today calls to mind the heroic story of Esther, but logic dictates that her behavior be examined for what it really was.

In the beginning, she was a beautiful young virgin who married outside her faith. It must be assumed that she had no choice. The king's harem was not a place a girl refused when the king was almost without any limitations on his authority. It might be argued that Esther should have refused to marry outside her faith, but she was a captive in Persia. Her choices seem to have been nil unless she chose to hide, and that seems impossible in a land where her people were exiled. She did what she had to do in that case, so we turn to other events to study the kind of woman she was.

In her early days, Esther was obedient to her older cousin and the chief eunuch. She listened to advice. She prepared for the presentation before the king so that she would be her best. She was. She was not like most of the virgins who visited the king once and then were sent back to the luxurious exile of the harem. Esther pleased the king and became his queen.

She knew her place and kept in the marriage until she had a choice to make. She hid her Jewish faith from the king. Now all Jews were to be killed at Haman's order.

At first, Esther wanted to continue her secret. She thought she would escape the purge until Mordecai warned her that this was not likely. In making her choice, Esther was willing to face the king on behalf of her people and the faith, even if she perished.

Esther's good graces with the king in the past paid off. She escaped the ever-ready headsmen at the throne. Esther, prepared through fasting and cooperation of her people, succeeded in getting her wish. Wisely, she didn't blurt out her request in front of the whole court, but sought a private audience with the king and the Jews' enemy, Haman.

Still, Esther bided her time. For whatever reason, she didn't make her move the first night, but held off. Noticeable in the Scriptures is that during that delay, several things happened that assured Esther's success the second banquet night.

The hardest part of Esther's personality to understand comes in her request to have the sons of Haman hanged. It is much easier to understand the Jews' defending themselves when it is understood that the king himself could not reverse his earlier order.

The celebration afterward commemorates the Jews' escaping genocide, though many thousands of them died in the fighting. Esther cannot be blamed for the slaughter or the natural inclination to want to celebrate deliverance.

Nevertheless, Esther is somewhat tarnished by her request to have Haman's sons hanged. She is still a hero to her people, but the Esther of her late twenties is a somewhat different woman from the young virgin introduced early in the story.

Perhaps there is something still hidden to us in the fact that nowhere in the book of Esther is there a single mention of God, prayers, or anything more spiritual than fasting. There is absolutely no hint of spiritual values or involvement in Esther's life.

So, while she was a wise, patient, obedient, and likable woman, Esther's heroism is somewhat dimmed by her own unexplainable act of hanging the sons of her people's great enemy.

Esther remains a multifaceted woman and an example of what can happen when a good personality is scarred by one abusive act of power. Her good still outweighs the bad, but it's sad that one inhuman act leaves us with a flawed image of an otherwise beautiful and heroic woman of her people.

1. Josephus, *Antiquities of the Jews,* p. 238.
2. Ibid.
3. Ibid.

EVE
REFERENCES: Genesis 2:21-25; 3:1-24; 4:1-2, 25;
2 Corinthians 11:13; 1 Timothy 2:13
SCRIPTURAL SYNOPSIS:

In the dawn of time, God saw that it was not good for the man,
Adam, to be alone, so the first woman was created from the man's
rib. She was tempted of Satan, in the guise of a serpent. The
woman ate forbidden fruit and gave some to her husband. Both of
them were exiled from the Garden of Eden.

After separation from God's presence, the woman was named
Eve. She bore the first child, Cain, and then his brother, Abel. A
third son, Seth, was later born, from whose descendants came
Jesus the Christ.

COMMENTARY:

Even people who have not read the Bible could give a fairly
comprehensive account of Eve's origin, her home and children,
plus the encounter with temptation which brought exclusion from
Paradise. But that's the shell of Eve — what was she like as a
woman who had feelings, emotions, and human characteristics
which mean something today?

What was it like to be the first and only woman in the world?

Eve wasn't born. She had no childhood, no memories of mother
and father, sisters or brothers — no past at all.

She just *was*.

The Bible explains that God had made the earth and heavens
and all in them. He had made man, called Adam, out of the
ground and breathed the breath of life into his nostrils. Adam
named the animals and did other solo things. But he had no mate,
as all of the beasts did.

"So the Lord God caused a deep sleep to fall upon the man,
and he slept; then He took one of his ribs, and closed up the flesh
at that place. And the Lord God fashioned into a woman the rib
which He had taken from the man, and brought her to the man"
(Gen. 2:22).

Adam, as the man had been identified only a couple of verses
before, said,

"This is now bone of my bones, and flesh of my flesh; she

shall be called Woman, because she was taken out of Man''
(2:23).

The Bible added, ''For this cause a man shall leave his father
and his mother, and shall cleave to his wife; and they shall become
one flesh. And the man and his wife were naked and were not
ashamed'' (2:24-25).

So we meet Eve, unborn, first woman in the world, made of a
rib and called woman. Not Eve. Just Woman. Man and wife were
nude and unashamed in the purity of their paradise.

A thoughtful sideline is that as soon as Adam hailed the new
creation as Woman, the Scriptures declare a man shall leave his
father and mother and become one flesh with his wife. Yet neither
Adam nor the Woman had parents to leave!

God, in His guidance of the Bible's preparation, allowed that
wording of the present-day wedding ceremony to be inserted at
the very beginning of the very first husband-wife relationship.

Evil is personified in the serpent, ''more crafty than any beast
of the field which the Lord God had made'' (3:1).

In this account, the serpent can talk although none of the other
creatures can. He says to the Woman, ''Indeed, has God said,
'You shall not eat from any tree of the garden?' ''

The Woman explained what she had probably heard from her
husband, since the edict was handed down before her time. They
could eat the fruit of any garden tree, except from ''the fruit of the
tree which is in the middle of the garden.'' God had said, ''You
shall not eat from it or touch it, lest you die'' (3:3).

The serpent replied, ''You surely shall not die!'' Perhaps the
Woman detected a hint of scorn in the speaker's voice. ''For God
knows,'' the serpent continued, ''that in the day you eat from it
your eyes will be opened, and you will be like God, knowing
good and evil'' (3:5).

The Woman listened to this thought-provoking declaration. So
she took a look at the tree. She saw that the tree was good for
food, was delightful to see, and was desirable to make one wise.
Satan made it all sound very logical and innocent.

The fruit as food had eye appeal. But the third feature of the
forbidden fruit causes some reflection. The Woman would be like

God, knowing good and evil. Up to this point, there is no suggestion she knew anything but good, because everything was perfect. Except for the serpent, no evil existed.

Human nature urged taking the forbidden thing.

The Woman took the fruit, ate it, and gave some to her husband, who also ate it.

A simple act. But what consequences!

"Then the eyes of both of them were opened, and they knew that they were naked; and they sewed fig leaves together and made themselves loin coverings" (3:7).

We're not told the Woman's thoughts or emotions. The Bible does not say she was sorry she disobeyed God. We don't know if she was sorry she listened to the serpent's seemingly rational temptation. We do know that her husband expressed the Scripture's first recorded human emotion: "I was afraid because I was naked, so I hid myself" (3:10).

The same feeling seems to have gripped the Woman, for she had also hidden when God approached. The first human emotion, then, is recorded as fear — and fear of God for disobedience.

God questioned Adam on what he had done. The husband promptly blamed his wife. God questioned the Woman. She blamed the serpent who had deceived her.

Her thoughts can be imagined. There had been an ideal situation. But because of one infraction of the rule — the only rule — God's judgment was pronounced.

God cursed the serpent. He put "enmity" between the serpent and the Woman; between her seed and the serpent's seed.

God then turned to the Woman. "I will greatly multiply your pain in childbirth, in pain you shall bring forth children; yet your desire shall be for your husband, and he shall rule over you" (3:16).

To this point, the narrative had not mentioned children. None has been born. And nothing has been said about the husband-wife relationship to show that it was anything except equal; now the husband would be her head; she would be subject to him.

The Woman's emotions must have been intense. She had done such a simple thing! The first biblical conversation ever recorded with the Woman had been with the serpent. There's no record of anything she and her husband had talked about. The serpent's words had seemed innocent enough. So she'd eaten this unnamed fruit from a forbidden tree. But the backlash was terrible for her.

God turned His judgment on the man who had listened to his wife and eaten the forbidden fruit. God's curse fell upon Adam.

At this point, the Woman is first named. Following the cursing by God, the Scriptures chose to include this line: "Now the man called his wife's name Eve, because she was the mother of all the living" (3:20).

If there is some significance to naming the woman at this time, it is not clear. Eve was not yet the "mother of all living," for the Scriptures had not talked of the children from Adam's and Eve's union.

There's no record on whether Eve wanted to cry out at the severity of God's punishment. We don't know if she realized it wasn't eating the fruit that had caused God's curse. It was her disobedience. The Bible does not say if she realized the sin was yielding to temptation, or disobedience, which brought the reprimand of God upon man, woman, and serpent. Eve may have wanted to lash out at the serpent. She might have wanted more punishment for the serpent. It was he who had been the one to encourage her to do a forbidden thing.

God made garments for Adam and his wife and then drove them from the garden. Cherubim (plural of cherub, a symbolic form of living creatures) were stationed to keep the couple out of the garden. A flaming sword, turning every way, guarded — not the garden — but "the way to the Tree of Life" (3:24).

Every woman who has been ejected from her home, her country, or other place of seeming security can suffer with Eve the anguish of dispossession. All that was good was suddenly lost. Man and wife were turned out to seek new directions, new goals, and a new home. But worst of all was the broken relationship with God.

The Scriptures don't tell us how Eve felt, or how she adjusted to the terrible blow which had fallen upon her, except in the hint of a possible new relationship.

The banishment record is immediately followed by the declaration, "Now the man had relations with his wife, Eve, and she conceived and gave birth to Cain, and she said, 'I have gotten a manchild with the help of the Lord'" (4:1).

Something of Eve's post-garden attitude is seen in her crediting the Lord's help in the birth of her first baby.

Eve bore another son, Abel. We're not told anything about how she felt holding her first-born and his brother. We're not told how she dealt with the emotions of seeing children grow up and with all the joys and problems related to being a family.

The Scriptures don't take long in showing what happened when Cain and Abel grew up. They both offered gifts to the Lord, something their parents are not said to have previously done. There was sibling rivalry over God's favoring Abel's gift, so Cain killed his younger brother.

The Scriptures don't tell us how this first mother reacted when her first-born son killed her only other child. The Bible follows the reaction of God to Cain and the resulting curse which drove the surviving son away to be a vagrant and a wanderer.

Eve's mental suffering must have been intense. Once she had lived in a garden of perfection. Once she and her husband had been able to personally hear the Lord walking through the garden and talking with them. Once Eve had two sons; now she had none. The household was silent and childless again.

The pain of the first mother can still be felt down through the centuries. She had lost one son to death and the other to banishment, perhaps never again to see his face. A mother without children; a woman with the memories of one son murdered by another and the memory of a living son driven out from her sight would have crushed anyone with heavy, depressing blackness of spirit. Could Eve have been different?

A brief verse shows God's mercy to the bereft woman called Eve. She had a third son, Seth. Again, Eve's attitude toward God is shown in her explaining the choice of the child's name.

"God has appointed me another offspring in place of Abel; for Cain killed him" (4:25).

With those words, Eve vanishes from the biblical scene. The New Testament makes a couple of references to her. "But I am afraid," Paul wrote in 2 Corinthians 11:3, "lest as the serpent deceived Eve by his craftiness, your minds should be led astray from the simplicity and purity of devotion to Christ."

Paul again refers to Eve in the epistle to Timothy, showing why he (Paul) would not allow a woman to teach or exercise authority over a man, but to remain quiet. "For it was Adam who was first created, and then Eve. And it was not Adam who was deceived, but the woman being quite deceived, fell into transgression" (1 Tim. 2:13-14).

So Eve, thousands of years after her third child was born and she is forgotten in the rest of the Old Testament, is used by Paul as an example. She was created after Adam, she was deceived, and she transgressed. Paul's condemnation is implied, and his attitude is still reflected in much of today's society.

No one should study Eve's story without identifying with the woman whose single indiscretion, no matter how slight it might have seemed to her at the moment, cost her everything, including her reputation.

Even her third son's name and importance are often overlooked. Almost no one seems to remember that it was from Seth that Luke traces the genealogy of Jesus the Christ. Seth, born out of Eve's terrible human tragedies, is a name not nearly as well known as the killer, Cain, and the victim, Abel. But God remembered, and out of Eve, mother of all people, came the seed that culminated in the brightest hope for mankind, the Prince of Peace.

HAGAR/AGAR
REFERENCES: Genesis 16:1, 3, 8, 15-16; 21:9, 14, 17; 25:12; Galatians 4:24-25.
SCRIPTURAL SYNOPSIS:

Hagar was an Egyptian maid to Sarah, who gave the woman to her husband, Abraham, to bear children for her. Jealousy arose when Hagar conceived, and the barren Sarah had her ejected from the camp. God intervened, Hagar returned to Sarah's service, bore a son, Ishmael, who it seemed would be Abraham's heir. When Ishmael was about thirteen, Sarah ejected Hagar, this time with her son, into the wilderness. She and the boy survived when God called from heaven, promised that Ishmael would become a great nation, and provided water for the dying child. Both survived. Hagar took an Egyptian wife for her son. Hagar is not mentioned again in the Old Testament.

COMMENTARY:

Hagar is first introduced in Genesis 16:1: "Now Sarai, Abram's wife, had borne him no children, and she had an Egyptian maid whose name was Hagar."

Sarai, later called Sarah, gave her slave-girl to her husband, later called Abraham, to bear a child for him. According to the custom of the times, any child born to Hagar would become the child of Sarah.

Abram had lived ten years in Canaan when he took Hagar. She became pregnant and immediately despised her mistress.

Sarai complained to her husband about her maid's attitude. Abram refused to get involved, saying the maid was in his wife's power: "Do to her what is good in your sight" (Gen. 6:6).

Sarai treated Hagar so harshly, the pregnant slave fled into the wilderness in violation of cultural laws about runaway slaves.

However, it wasn't a slave-hunter from Abram's and Sarai's camp who found the pregnant woman, but an angel of the Lord. This is the first Old Testament record of an angelic visit to a woman.

As the slave paused by a wilderness spring of water, perhaps as the fugitive fled toward her homeland in Egypt, the angel demanded, "Where have you come from and where are you going?" (Gen. 16:8).

"I am fleeing from the presence of my mistress Sarai."

"Return to your mistress, and submit yourself to her authority" (16:9).

The Scriptures don't say, but the slave woman must have been concerned by such a suggestion. The angel had asked where Hagar came from, but anyone of such non-earthly background must have known what the slave knew. Hagar's emotions must have been high enough that she might have blurted out that the angel didn't know what he was saying.

Sarai had proved to be a harsh woman, forcing a pregnant slave girl out into the wilderness. But Sarai's frustrations were understandable. She was Abram's half-sister and wife who had come from Ur in the land of Mesopotamia. God had promised Abram a son, but after at least ten years in Canaan, plus some time spent in Egypt, where Hagar was probably obtained, Sarai was still barren. She had given her slave to bear a child, and then, when the child was conceived, resented Hagar's smug attitude. To return to the authority of such a mistress must have appeared dangerous.

After all, Sarai was seventy-six years old. She had remained such a great beauty that even a few years earlier, in her mid-sixties, two men had wanted her in their harems. Abram had permitted it, claiming Sarai was his sister, which was true. But Sarai was childless and not getting any younger. If Hagar returned to such a mistress, both the slave and her son could expect continued problems. Abram was about eighty-five years old, and he'd have his son by a pregnant slave girl. This wouldn't make his bitter, childless wife, Sarai, the kind of woman Hagar wanted to be around.

Hagar's feelings aren't given, but the humanness of this Egyptian so far from home must have been mixed with disbelief at what the angel told her. Still, Hagar listened as the angel continued.

"I will greatly multiply your descendants so they shall be too many to count" (16:10).

The angel told Hagar the child she was carrying would be a son. She was to name him Ishmael, meaning "God hears," because the Lord had seen Hagar's affliction. But Ishmael "will be a wild donkey of a man, his hand will be against everyone, and everyone's hand will be against him; and he will live to the east of his brothers" (16:12).

Hagar's thoughts at those words can be imagined. What mother wants a wild man, whose hand is against everyone, and everyone is against him? And how could he live east of his brothers, since he had none?

The Bible is silent on Hagar's thoughts. The Scriptures simply say, "Then she called the name of the Lord who spoke to her, 'Thou art a God who sees,' for she said, 'Have I even remained alive here after seeing Him?'"

Although Hagar had come from the land of gods far different from the one God Abram worshiped, she had apparently picked up a belief in God. She equated the angel with God and was surprised to find that she had lived after seeing Him.

Hagar's encounter with the angel took place at a well called Beer-lahai-roi, or "the well of the living one who sees me."

Hagar returned to Sarai's service. Hagar bore a son, and Abram named the boy Ishmael, as Hagar had been ordered by the angel.

The Scriptures are silent on the kind of treatment Hagar received during the next several years. Sarai remained childless until Ishmael was about thirteen years old.

Abram was ninety-nine when the Lord changed his name to Abraham (Exalted Father) and Sarai was henceforth known as Sarah (Princess, Mistress). The covenant of circumcision was started. And, not long afterward, Abraham and Sarah had a son, Isaac. Hagar's troubles with her mistress again flared up shortly thereafter.

The conflict exploded when Isaac was weaned at about age three. Ishmael, then about seventeen, and his mother were seen by Sarah "mocking," or teasing, the weaning Isaac.

Sarah's jealousy showed in her demand of Abraham, "Drive out this maid and her son, for the son of this maid shall not be an heir with my son Isaac" (Gen. 21:10).

The Bible says this distressing request caused the father to seek counsel of the Lord. The unbelievable answer was, "Do not be distressed because of the lad and your maid; whatever Sarah tells you, listen to her, for through Isaac your descendants shall be named. And of the son of the maid, I will make a nation also, because he is your descendant" (21:13).

For the second time, Hagar was thrown out into the desert. This time, she had her teenage son with only some bread and a skin of water for survival.

Again, Hagar wandered in the wilderness of Beersheba. In time, the inevitable happened. The water was used up. Death seemed certain. We can feel for this Egyptian mother as she left her son under some bushes and sat down opposite him, a bowshot away. The Scriptures say Hagar spoke.

Hagar said, "Do not let me see the boy die" (21:16).

We can logically suppose Hagar was doubting the angelic announcement of about eighteen years before. It seems she might have been losing her faith. God had promised to multiply her descendants so they would be too numerous to count. God had promised Abraham a nation from Hagar. But now the link to those uncounted descendants was about to be broken; the son lay dying of thirst in the desert, and his mother was powerless. She despaired. When he died, God's promise died with him. Then only death was left for Hagar.

It was in this moment of total helplessness, total vulnerability, total resignation, that God's promise was revitalized. The promises of God often are fulfilled when human means are at an end.

The Scriptures don't say God heard Hagar's plea not to see the boy die. Instead, we're told, "God heard the lad crying; and the angel of God called to Hagar out of heaven" (Gen. 21:17).

There was a firm reprimand for her loss of faith. "What is the matter with you, Hagar?" Then came the reassurance. "Do not fear, for God has heard the voice of the lad where he is. Arise, lift up the lad, and hold him by the hand; for I will make a great nation of him" (21:18).

God opened Hagar's eyes. She saw a well of water, filled the skin, and gave the boy a drink.

We're not told of the joy Hagar must have felt, but anyone who has ever sat by a dying child can identify with the surging hope which raced through her mind.

The Scriptures give us only one brief comment after Hagar gave water to her dying son. "And God was with the lad, and he grew; and he lived in the wilderness, and became an archer. And he lived in the wilderness, and Paran; and his mother took a wife for him from the land of Egypt" (21:20-21).

Hagar's story ends happily, we assume, for she chose her son's bride from her own people. And that raises some fascinating possibilities and questions.

Was Hagar disappointed and bitter over her son's father allowing them to be thrust out into the wilderness to die alone? Was her choice of an Egyptian daughter-in-law a slap at the Hebrew patriarch who had fathered her son? Was this act by Hagar a repudiation of all that she had learned in the tents of Abraham and Sarah?

We don't know, but millions of Muslims today trace their ancestry through Abraham and Hagar. So we can sense some possibility that the slave girl and her son were not friendly to the faith of Abraham. Paul the apostle wrote that the Children of Israel came from Abraham and Sarah through Isaac, and, by faith, so did the Christians. Hagar and her son were allegorical to another line of faith.

God's intervention in Hagar's life, however, suggests some possibilities. Since He is a God of order, and His plans were laid before the foundation of the earth, can this strange story of Hagar have any possible bearing on what the New Testament declares will eventually happen at the end of the world battle of Armageddon?

It is not too farfetched. According to millions of people around the world, their ancestors came through the tribe of Ishmaelites, northern Arabian nomads. Muhammed is said to have descended from the Arabs of the union of Hagar and Abraham. The followers of Muhammed, whose religion is called Islam, today (as a newspaper headline put it) have the rest of the world over an oil barrel.

The angel at Hagar's first visitation had told her the unborn child in her womb would be a wild man. He would live to the east of his brothers, and everyone's hand would be against him, and his hand against them.

For centuries after the rise of Islam, descendants of Hagar's son defeated the followers of Christ. For centuries, the followers of Muhammed held much of the Christian's holy land; land that is also sacred to the Jews, of whom Abraham was the direct ancestor.

Not until 1967 did the Jews regain their sacred sites in Jerusalem, some eighteen hundred years after they were first lost to the Romans and then later held by those who trace their ancestors to Ishmael and Hagar.

There had been no serious religious war in hundreds of years, but the militant call of Iran's Ayatollah Khomeini for Muslims to arm themselves against the Christians came as a cold blade of steel through the world's peace.

Could it blow over? Yes. But if it doesn't, could the whole thing have started with Hagar, whose mistress and master ostracized her nearly four thousand years ago?

HANNAH
REFERENCES: 1 Samuel 1:1-28; 2:1-10, 19-21
SCRIPTURAL SYNOPSIS:

Hannah was the barren wife of Elkanah, whose other wife had sons and daughters. Hannah prayed for a son, vowing she would give him to the Lord if God granted her petition. The prayer was answered and a son, Samuel, was born. Hannah dedicated the boy to the Lord for life and surrendered him at a young age to minister to the Lord under the direction of Eli the priest. Hannah yearly provided Samuel with a robe as he served God. Hannah had other children after she kept her vow to the Lord.

COMMENTARY:

Hannah was married to Elkanah, from the hill country of Ephraim. Elkanah's other wife was Peninnah, who had sons and daughters and tormented Hannah because she was childless. In that society and culture, no greater heartbreak could be borne by a wife than to be barren.

The situation was made worse because the husband showed by his actions and words that he loved Hannah more than his other wife.

Each year, Elkanah went to Shiloh to worship and sacrifice to God. When Elkanah sacrificed, he gave portions to Peninnah and all her children, but Elkanah gave Hannah a double portion because he loved her, "But the Lord had closed her womb."

The other wife bitterly provoked and irritated Hannah because of her barrenness. It got to be so bad a situation that each year, when Hannah went up to the Lord's house, she couldn't eat because she wept so much over her situation.

Hannah's husband said, "Hannah, why do you weep? Why do you not eat? Why is your heart sad? Am I not better to you than ten sons?" (1 Sam. 1:8).

Hannah's answer isn't recorded. She finished eating and drinking at Shiloh, then went near the temple of the Lord. There, greatly distressed, she wept bitterly and prayed. But she spoke only in her heart. Her lips moved, but her voice wasn't audible.

Eli the priest saw her from his position at a seat by the temple doorpost. Seeing the woman's lips move but not hearing anything, he assumed she was drunk. He approached her.

By then, Hannah had silently made a vow. "O Lord of hosts, if Thou wilt indeed look on the affliction of Thy maidservant and remember me, and not forget Thy maidservant, but wilt give Thy maidservant a son, then I will give him to the Lord all the days of his life, and a razor shall never come on his head" (1 Sam. 1:11).

But Eli the priest, looking only at the woman's outward appearance of silently moving lips, upbraided her. "How long will you make yourself drunk? Put away the wine!" (1:14).

Hannah replied, "No, my Lord, I am a woman oppressed in spirit; I have drunk neither wine nor strong drink, but I have poured out my soul before the Lord.

"Don't consider your maidservant as a worthless woman; for I have spoken until now out of my great concern and provocation" (1:15-16).

Eli answered, "Go in peace; and may the God of Israel grant your petition that you have asked of Him" (1:17).

Hannah arose, ate, and went her way. But she was no longer sad.

The family got up early the next morning, worshiped the Lord, and returned to their home. Elkanah had relations with Hannah, "and the Lord remembered her" (1:19).

She conceived and bore a son whom she named Samuel, saying, "Because I have asked him of the Lord" (1:20).

Elkanah and the rest of his household went to offer the Lord his yearly sacrifice and pay his vow, but Hannah did not accompany Elkanah.

"I will not go up until the child is weaned," Hannah explained. "Then I will bring him, that he may appear before the Lord and stay there forever" (1:22).

Elkanah replied, "Do what seems best to you. Remain here until you have weaned him; only may the Lord confirm His word" (1:23).

When Samuel was weaned, Hannah took him to the house of the Lord in Shiloh. Hannah brought along a three-year-old bull, a jug of wine, and one ephah of flour (about two-thirds of a bushel, dry measure).

The boy's age isn't given, but he is described as "young." It's known that Hebrew mothers of Samuel's time usually weaned a child at age two or three.

The sacrificial bull was slaughtered, and the boy was brought to Eli the priest. Hannah said to him, "Oh, my lord! As your soul lives, my lord, I am the woman who stood here beside you, praying to the Lord. For this boy I prayed, and the Lord has given me my petition which I asked of Him.

"So I have also dedicated him to the Lord. As long as he lives, he is dedicated to the Lord" (1:26-28).

Then Hannah prayed in somewhat the same way Mary, mother of Jesus, did centuries later in what is called the Magnificat.

"My heart exults in the Lord; my horn is exalted in the Lord, my mouth speaks boldly against my enemies, because I rejoice in Thy salvation.

"There is no one holy like the Lord, indeed, there is no one besides Thee, nor is there any rock like our God" (1 Sam. 2:2).

The new mother's song of praise continues for another eight verses, but there is no mention of her son or the sacrifice she was making. Hannah simply praised God for who He was. Then she left her small son, who "ministered to the Lord before Eli the priest" (2:11).

Year by year, Hannah made a little robe for her son and brought it to Samuel when the family came to offer the yearly sacrifice (2:19).

"Then Eli would bless Elkanah and his wife and say, 'May the Lord give you children from this woman in place of the one she has dedicated to the Lord'" (2:21).

Hannah had five more children to grow up about her skirts while her oldest child served the Lord (2:21).

Hannah's name is not again mentioned in Scripture. Her work was done. She had given her first-born to the Lord, and the Lord would use Samuel in a mighty way.

It is a fascinating study in human nature, for Hannah's conflicting emotions can be imagined. Once she had a child, she could have thought about breaking her vow. Hannah's reasons can easily find identification today.

She could have thought, "I can't give Samuel up! I know what I promised God, but I can't do it. What if I never have another child? What will my husband say? After all, the boy's his, too. He's the head of the household. I have no right to make such a decision on my own."

Hannah could have reasoned that it was unfair to wrest the young boy from the arms of his parents and leave him with the old priest. Eli's own sons were certainly not good examples for a young boy. Hannah could have rightly been concerned with how the boy would feel in strange surroundings. He might not understand that his mother was keeping a vow to God. The child would, on the other hand, understand he had been taken from his home and given into the care of another. Perhaps he would reason that his mother didn't love him and was giving him away. Who could be depended upon to properly care for a small boy in the temple?

It is possible that all these thoughts crossed Hannah's mind. They are very much the kinds of things a modern mother might think about her only son.

But the Scriptures give no indication that any such thoughts entered Hannah's mind. There's no hint that she tried to reason her way out of her vow, thinking, "I'll keep the boy until he's grown. Or at least in his teens. Then I'll give him to the Lord. After all, what good can a small boy be to God? Yes, that's what I'll do: I'll give Samuel to the Lord, but later. That's not breaking my vow."

Hannah, however, was obedient. She asked for a son. She got the child. She kept her vow. God honored Hannah's faithfulness with more children, and Samuel grew up to be one of the Old Testament's most important men.

LEAH

REFERENCES: Genesis 29:16-32; 30:1-21; 31:4, 33; 33:2-7; 34:1; 35:23-26; 46:15; 49:31; Ruth 4:11

SCRIPTURAL SYNOPSIS:

Leah was the oldest daughter of Laban and sister to the much-prettier Rachel. Jacob loved the younger sister, but their father defrauded Jacob and gave him Leah for a wife. Jacob also married Rachel. The two daughters of Laban gave their maids to Jacob to bear children for them. Leah's maid was Zilpah.

Leah, always seeking her husband's favor over her beautiful sister, bore Jacob four sons, Reuben, Simeon, Levi, and Judah, before giving her maid to Jacob. Later, Leah also bore Jacob sons, Issachar and Zebulun, and a daughter, Dinah. Leah's maid bore sons Gad and Asher.

While her beautiful younger sister lived, Leah took second place in her husband's favors. There was strife between the sisters.

Leah's adventures included being placed ahead of her sister and her son when their husband thought his wronged brother, Esau, was coming to attack the families. If that had happened, Leah and her children would have been killed before the vengeful brother got to Rachel and her child.

Eventually, Leah outlived her sister and seemingly was favored enough of her husband that he buried her with his famous parents, Isaac and Rebekah, and Jacob's grandparents, Abraham and Sarah.

From Leah's fourth-born son, Judah, came the line which gave the Jews their name and produced King David and Joseph, husband of Mary, who bore Jesus.

COMMENTARY:

The Bible introduces Leah when her younger shepherdess sister brings home Jacob, their cousin. His mother was Rebekah, who had married Isaac, Abraham's son. Rebekah was a sister to Laban, the Syrian or Arameanian, Leah's and Rachel's father. Leah and her family lived in Paddan-aram northeast of the Euphrates River. Leah had some brothers whose names are unknown.

Leah's father was a deceitful man. This caused Leah's first problem, which developed into a twenty year series of problems.

Leah is a prototype, a plain-looking woman with a beautiful

sister. Except for her eyes, there was nothing especially noticeable about her. The visiting cousin, Jacob, fell in love with Rachel and said he would serve seven years in place of a dowry. Laban agreed, but when the wedding night came, the deceitful father substituted Leah.

The switch poses some difficulties in understanding how a marriage was performed in the days of the Hebrew partriarchs.

Leah may have also loved the cousin who had fled from his vengeful brother, Esau, whom Jacob had defrauded. Leah apparently had no rights of her own, for her father had to slip her into Jacob's tent on the wedding night. Leah went at her father's orders.

Her thoughts are not revealed, but they can be imagined. The man with whom she shared the nuptial tent had loved and been promised her beautiful sister. Leah and Jacob consummated a marriage that obviously had not been a formal one before witnesses, as we understand a ceremony. Leah's husband must have been celebrating somewhat before entering the tent, for otherwise he would have known the woman with whom he was sleeping for the first time was not Rachel.

It was only in the morning that Jacob realized he had the wrong wife. He protested to his new father-in-law. Laban explained that in his country it was the practice for the older daughter to marry first. However, Laban said, if Jacob would complete the wedding week with Leah, Jacob could also have Rachel for another seven years of service.

With two sisters sharing the same husband, troubles weren't long in developing. The Bible says, "The Lord saw that Leah was unloved, and He opened her womb, but Rachel was barren" (Gen. 29:31).

We learn something of Leah's faith in God when she bore each son. When the first was born, she named him Reuben because "the Lord has seen my affliction; surely now my husband will love me" (29:32).

When Simeon was born to her, she said, "Because the Lord has heard that I am unloved, He has therefore given me this son also."

By the time Levi, the third son, was born, Leah's thoughts had seemingly given up on love, for she used a milder term in saying, "Now this time my husband will become attached to me, because I have borne him three sons" (29:34).

The progression of declining hope for love was evident when her fourth son was born, for now Leah shifted emphasis from her husband. "This time I will praise the Lord." She named this son Judah. Then she stopped bearing.

By now, Leah's beautiful sister was jealous because Leah had four sons and she was barren. Leah may have overheard the angry exchange between her pretty sister and their husband which led Rachel to give her maid, Bilhah, to Jacob to bear children by the servant girl.

Bilhah bore to Jacob, Dan and then Naphtali. The second birth revealed more of Leah's problems with Rachel. The pretty sister declared, "With mighty wrestlings I have wrestled with my sister, and I have indeed prevailed" (30:8). In those few words, the Scriptures show that Leah had suffered at least six years of sibling rivalry while sharing the same husband.

Leah's sister considered that the children born to her maid were really hers, an interesting insight into the culture in which Leah lived.

Leah, believing she was not going to have any more children, also gave her maid, Zilpah, to Jacob. Since Jacob and Leah already had four sons, this action suggests Leah believed she would give her husband more children through the custom of maidservants as substitute mothers.

Another insight into the human feelings of Leah is shown in how the birth of two sons to her maid made Leah feel. With Zilpah's first-born, Leah exclaimed, "How fortunate!" The boy was called Gad. The second birth by the maid caused Leah to say, "Happy am I! For women will call me happy." Leah — not Zilpah — named the boy Asher (Gen. 30:11-13).

Leah had given up saying things about her husband loving her, or praising God, for now she was looking at her own feelings. Zilpah's sons, as Leah's, were fortunate and happy for her because women would say Leah was happy.

The shift in emphasis from love and God to self may be partly explained in the next scriptural incident. Reuben, Leah's oldest son, gathered some mandrakes in the wheat harvest time. He presented the mandrakes to his mother. Rachel asked her sister for some of the mandrakes.

Leah replied, "It is a small matter for you to take my husband? And would you take my son's mandrakes also?"

Rachel replied that Jacob could sleep that night with Leah in exchange for the mandrakes. The agreement was made. Leah approached Jacob that evening as he came in from the fields.

"You must come in to me tonight," Leah said, "for I have hired you with my son's mandrakes" (Gen. 30:16).

This shows that Leah had been surplanted in her husband's life to such an extent he wasn't even sleeping with her any more. Apparently Rachel had something to say about that, for the incident shows how desperate Leah was for her husband's attentions, and how deeply divided she and Rachel were.

The union resulted in a fifth son whom Leah named Issachar. She also conceived and bore a sixth son, Zebulun. Later, she had a daughter, Dinah.

Leah's position in the marriage had deteriorated so badly that she was reduced to hiring her own husband away from her sister. But once Jacob began sleeping with Leah again, the relationship continued about three more years.

At last Leah's sister became pregnant. Leah must have wondered how her husband would treat her now that she had borne him six sons and a daughter, plus two sons by her maid — and Rachel was about to have her first child. Leah would have to wait and see.

All this time, Jacob had been serving his wives' father. Jacob had served a total of fourteen years for the Syrian's daughters and six years for some livestock. God had blessed Jacob, but Laban's flocks had diminished. Leah's and Rachel's unnamed brothers protested to their father that Jacob was cheating them out of their inheritance.

Laban's attitude changed toward Leah's husband. Jacob called Leah and Rachel to him and explained their father's changed behavior. He then announced that God had told him to return to his own land.

Leah listened with her sister as their husband explained in

detail how God had taken away their father's livestock and given it
to Jacob, and how he was instructed by an angel to leave their
homeland for his.

In a rare display of harmony, Leah and Rachel spoke. "Do we
still have any portion or inheritance in our father's house? Are we
not reckoned to him as foreigners? For he has sold us, and has
also entirely consumed our purchase price.

"Surely," the sisters concluded, "all the wealth which God
has taken away from our father belongs to us and our children;
now then, do whatever God has said to you" (31:14-16).

The scriptural attribution of this conversation to Leah and Rachel
suggests that perhaps a better relationship existed between them
since Rachel had borne a son, Joseph. But Jacob's clear choice of
Rachel over Leah still remained in what happened on the trip to
Canaan.

Laban pursued Jacob, for someone from his family had stolen
Laban's household idols. Jacob didn't know that Rachel had been
the thief. The Scriptures don't tell us whether or not Leah knew
her sister was guilty.

Laban caught up with Jacob, searched his tent first, then Leah's,
the maids', and finally Rachel's. The order of the search suggests
that even Leah's own father wasn't too fond of her, or at least that
he suspected her above anyone except Jacob.

When Laban failed to find the idols, Jacob confronted him
angrily. But God had warned Laban not to harm Jacob, and the
encounter ended peacefully. Jacob and his family moved on.

The second event on the road to Canaan again showed how
Leah was viewed by her husband. It had been twenty years since
Jacob had cheated his brother and fled Esau's wrath. But Jacob
sent presents and word he was coming. Esau responded by leading four hundred men toward Jacob.

Jacob prayed, sent more presents, and then took action. If Esau
attacked, he would first come to the maids and their children, then
Leah and her children, and finally, in the safest, farthest-back
position, would be Rachel and her son.

But Esau arrived with open arms and forgiveness for his twin
brother who had cheated him so long ago. Leah and her children

came after the two maids and their children to bow before Esau. Rachel and Joseph came last.

Leah was still a second-class wife after more than twenty years. Even in Canaan she was not to find the happiness she must have longed for. Her daughter, Dinah, was raped by Shechem, son of Hamor the Hivite. The girl's attacker was an uncircumcised worshiper of strange gods, which added to the anger of her brothers. Simeon and Levi deceived the men of Shechem, tricked them into being circumcised in hopes of marrying into Jacob's family, and then killed all the Shechemites while they were sore and unable to defend themselves.

When Leah's sons returned with all the booty they had seized after the massacre, Jacob berated the boys, who then defended their actions.

But the Scriptures don't tell us a thing about how Leah felt to have her daughter raped, two of her sons become mass murderers, and the threat of reprisal from Canaanites and Perizzites hanging ominously over her family. Leah lived through these tragedies and concerns in scriptural silence.

Leah's emotions are not recorded in the next major event in the household. As Jacob and his family journeyed from Shechem toward Bethel and then on toward Ephrath (Bethlehem), her beautiful younger sister died in childbirth. The baby, another boy, was named Benjamin.

Jacob buried Rachel on the way to Bethlehem. We wonder what Leah thought as she stood by her sister's grave. Her emotions must have been strong as Jacob raised a pillar over the grave and then journeyed on again. The Scriptures are silent on Leah's and his relationship during this period.

By now, Reuben, Leah's and Jacob's oldest son, was grown. He brought disgrace on his father by sleeping with Bilhah, who had been Rachel's maid. The scandal was widely known and caused the first-born son to lose his father's blessing.

Again, the Scriptures are silent on how Leah felt about this brazen and disrespectful act of her oldest son. But it undoubtedly caused more grief for Leah. Still, her troubles were not over.

There is little left of Leah's story, except one brief comment which tells us where she died and gives rise to our hope that there was a happy ending to her long story.

Famine struck the land. Over a period of time, Jacob's family was forced into Egypt. By then, Leah was a grandmother. She is mentioned in Genesis 46:15 but in such a way that it is not clear whether she went into Egypt with her descendants and husband. Her death is not detailed, but it was in Canaan.

Since Jacob blessed his sons as he was dying in Egypt and mentions Leah for the last time as already dead, it may be presumed that she did not go into Egypt. The final clue to this woman is found in Jacob's (then called Israel) recorded words of blessing on his sons.

"I am about to be gathered to my people; bury me with my fathers in the cave that is in the field of Ephron the Hittite, in the cave that is in the field of Machpelah, which is before Mamre, in the land of Canaan, which Abraham bought along with the field from Ephron the Hittite for a burial site.

"There they buried Abraham and his wife, Sarah, there they buried Isaac and his wife Rebekah, and there I buried Leah" (Gen. 49:29-31).

In our human wish for everything to have a happy ending, it is hoped that before Jacob buried Leah with his parents and grandparents, the couple had a final few years of happiness together. There is no scriptural confirmation for this view, but it seems logical.

Neither Leah nor Jacob was young any more. The beautiful younger sister and Jacob's favorite wife was dead in childbirth. Jacob and Leah had known enough of heartbreak and tragedy over their daughter and the vengeful action of her brothers. Jacob had thought his favorite son, Joseph, had been killed by wild animals. Later, he had learned that his own sons (including some of Leah's) had conspired to sell Joseph into Egyptian slavery. Some of Leah's sons had later found Joseph alive and in a position of power when famine drove the family out of Canaan into Egypt.

So Leah had known a lifetime of hard knocks. But in death, she slept with her husband in the family crypt near Hebron. The body of her beautiful sister wasn't there because Rachel had been buried on the road to Canaan when she died in childbirth.

Leah became one of the founding mothers of the house of Israel. She gave birth to half of the twelve sons who became the twelve tribes of Israel. So Leah rightfully takes her place with the matriarchs: Sarah, Rebekah, and Rachel.

The last Old Testament reference to Leah is in Ruth 4:11, where well-wishers tell Boaz — a direct descendant of Leah's Judah — that they trust Boaz's bride will be "like Rachel and Leah, both of whom built the house of Israel."

Centuries later, the younger sister's name is still ahead of Leah's. But even further on in the historical record, King David and Jesus Christ were counted from Leah's line, not her sister's.

MIRIAM
REFERENCES: Exodus 2:4-10; 15:20-21; Numbers 12:1-15; 20:1; 26:59; 1 Chronicles 6:3; Micah 6:4
SCRIPTURAL SYNOPSIS:

Miriam helped save her younger brother's life. He grew up to be the lawgiver, Moses. Miriam was a prophetess who sang praises to God when her brother successfully led their people out of Egyptian bondage and across the Red Sea. However, religious pride caused Miriam to join another brother, Aaron, in criticizing Moses. God struck Miriam with leprosy. She was healed upon Moses' prayer.

COMMENTARY:

Miriam was the oldest daughter of Amram and his wife, Jochobed. A second child, Aaron, was born before Pharoah decreed that all new-born Hebrew male children were to be killed. Moses, the third child, was born shortly after the decree was issued.

Although unnamed, Miriam enters the story when her mother could no longer hide her infant son, Moses. Jochebed made a watertight wicker basket and placed the three-month-old child in· it. The basket was then set among the reeds of the river, presumably the Nile.

Miriam, an apparently astute girl of perhaps twelve or so, stood where she could see what happened to the baby.

Pharoah's daughter came to bathe in the river, accompanied by her maidens. The princess saw the basket in the reeds. She ordered a maid to bring the basket. When it was opened, she saw the baby crying. The Egyptian had pity on the boy, recognizing him as a Hebrew.

Miriam approached Pharoah's daughter and said, "Shall I go and call a nurse for you from the Hebrew women, that she may nurse the child for you?" (Ex. 2:7)

"Go ahead," the princess said.

Miriam called her mother, who came to the Egyptian. The princess ordered Jochebed, "Take this child away and nurse him for me and I shall give you your wages" (2:9).

Jochebed took her son, nursed him, and then, when he was older, Jochebed brought him back to Pharoah's daughter. She named him Moses, saying, "Because I drew him out of the water" (2:10).

The Scriptures then concentrate on Moses' life, completely omitting anything more on his sister, Miriam, until after the Hebrews' flight across the Red Sea. However, to appreciate Miriam's later conflicts, it is necessary to understand something more of her youngest brother.

After Moses was rescued from death by the scripturally unnamed daughter of Pharoah (Josephus calls her Thermuthis), Moses was reared and educated an an Egyptian. He fled for his life after killing an Egyptian attacking a Hebrew. Moses settled in the land of Midian, married, and stayed in exile until God called him to re-enter Egypt and lead the Hebrews out of slavery.

We first hear of Miriam by name after Moses had led the Hebrews out of bondage and across the Red Sea. Aaron had acted as Moses' spokesman in Egypt. All three siblings had escaped ahead of Pharoah's pursuing chariots. The Red Sea parted miraculously, and the Hebrews crossed safely over on the first leg of their journey toward the Promised Land.

Miriam is introduced by name as "the prophetess, Aaron's sister." She took a timbrel (a kind of tambourine) and led the women in a dance (Ex. 15:20).

Miriam said, "Sing to the Lord, for He is highly exalted; the horse and his rider He has hurled into the sea'' (Ex. 15:21).

Miriam is not mentioned here as Moses' sister. As a prophetess, she was the feminine equivalent of a divinely inspired foreteller, but more accurately ''one who speaks for another,'' as the Hebrew word means.

Miriam is the first prohetess mentioned in the Old Testament. She held a position of high spiritual leadership among her people. Less than half a dozen other prophetesses are mentioned by name in the Bible, although the New Testament indicates they were more numerous.

The third time we hear of Miriam in Scriptures, she was in trouble. This started when she and Aaron spoke against Moses because of a Cushite (Ethiopian) woman Moses had married. However, the scriptural quotations show Miriam and Aaron really were suffering from injured spiritual pride.

''Has the Lord indeed spoken only through Moses? Has He not spoken through us as well?'' (Num. 12:2).

Moses was ''very humble, more than any man who was on the face of the earth'' (Num. 12:3). He didn't defend himself against his siblings' charges. But God intervened. He ordered all three to go to the tent of meeting. They obeyed. The Lord came down in a cloud pillar and stood at the tent's doorway. God called Miriam and Aaron who came forward as God spoke to them.

''Hear now My words: If there is a prophet among you, I the Lord shall make Myself known to him in a vision. I shall speak with him in a dream'' (Num. 12:6).

But Moses was more than a prophet, as God explained. ''Not so, with My servant, Moses. He is faithful in all My household. With him I will speak mouth to mouth, even openly, and not in dark sayings. And he beholds the form of the Lord'' (Num. 12:7-8).

God then demanded to know why Aaron and Miriam were not afraid to speak against ''My servant, against Moses?'' The issue was not verbal attacks on a younger brother but attacks against God's servant, Moses.

God's anger ''burned against'' Miriam and Aaron as the Lord departed. But Miriam alone was struck visibly.

When the cloud had withdrawn from the tent, Miriam was leprous.

Aaron pleaded with Moses, "Oh, my lord, I beg you, do not account this sin to us, in which we have acted foolishly and in which we have sinned. Oh, do not let her be like one dead, whose flesh is half eaten away when he comes from his mother's womb!" (Num. 12:11-12).

Moses cried to the Lord, "O God, heal her, I pray!" (12:13).

The Lord told Moses, "If her father had but spit in her face, would she not bear her shame for seven days? Let her be shut up for seven days outside the camp, and afterward she may be received again" (Num. 12:14).

It was Moses' prayer of intercession that removed Miriam's leprosy. She did not, or could not, plead to be relieved of her condition.

Miriam is last mentioned in the narrative of the Hebrews' journey to the Promised Land. "Then the sons of Israel, the whole congregation, came to the wilderness of Zin in the first month; and the people stayed at Kadesh. Now Miriam died there and was buried there" (Num. 20:1).

There is no mention of mourning for Miriam. It is not clear as to whether or not she had ever been restored to her previously high standing, but the implication is that she had not.

Her final mention in the Pentateuch (the first five books of the Bible) is given as a warning: "Remember what the Lord your God did to Miriam on the way as you came out of Egypt" (Deut. 24:9).

God had sent the three siblings to the Hebrews for His purpose, as the last mention of Miriam in the Old Testament shows. "Indeed, I brought you from the house of slavery, and I sent before you Moses, Aaron and Miriam" (Micah 6:4).

Miriam began as a very skillful young girl who probably saved the life of her infant brother. She rose to one of the highest religious positions in the community and then was stricken because of sibling rivalry and spiritual pride. She was restored to health, but apparently not to her former spiritual standing.

God's warning stands relevant today: Remember Miriam.

NAOMI
REFERENCES: book of Ruth
SCRIPTURAL SYNOPSIS:

Naomi lived in the days when judges ruled over the Hebrews. She was married to a Bethlehemite named Elimelech. The couple had two sons, Mahlon and Chilion. They were Ephratites, which was another name for their hometown of Bethlehem in Judea.

A famine forced the family to enter the country of Moab, where the sons married. Elimelech and both sons died. Naomi urged her daughters-in-law to return to their own people. Orpah, widow of Chilion, did so, but Ruth, Mahlon's widow, insisted on staying with Naomi. They journeyed back to Bethlehem, where Naomi guided Ruth into marrying Boaz. Out of this union came an ancestor to King David and, eventually, Joseph, husband of Mary, mother of Jesus Christ.

COMMENTARY:

The Bible hastily sketches in the background for the dramatic story that occupies most of the book of Ruth. The drama was in what happened after Naomi lost all three male members of her family in a foreign land.

It has been speculated that an epidemic took the lives of Naomi's husband and their two sons. The Bible does not say. But it was a terrible tragedy for a Hebrew woman to lose the male household members.

The Old Testament is filled with Hebrew prophets' denunciation of Moabites (Isa. 15, 16, 25; Jer. 9:26; 25:21; 27:3, 48; Ezek. 25:8-11; Amos 2:1-2; Zeph. 2:8-11). They were descended from the incestuous relationship of Lot and one of his daughters. The Moabites worshiped Chemosh, Ashtor-chemosh, and other fertility gods and goddesses. It wasn't until David's time that Israel subdued these people of such vastly different religious convictions.

It is understandable why Naomi and her husband had left the famine of Judea for Moab, however. The area was located east of Bethlehem, beyond the Dead Sea. It was a land of plentiful rain, lush vegetation, and large herds of sheep and cattle.

Naomi's feeling at her sons' marrying Moabite women isn't
given, but it can be imagined she felt somewhat as Rebecca and
Isaac had when Esau married Canaanite girls. Mahlon, mentioned
first, was presumably the older son. He married Ruth (Ruth 4:10).
Chilion had wed Orpah.

As the story opens, Naomi has made a decision. She'd heard
the famine was over in Bethlehem-Judea. She proposed to return
to her people. The Scriptures indicate that both daughters-in-law
started the journey with Naomi (1:7).

However, Naomi then suggested that both girls return to their
mother's house. The choice of ''mother's house'' indicates a
different perspective than the Hebrews had, in which the father's
house was a commonly used term.

Naomi's first recorded words, urging her daughters-in-law to
return to the homes of their mothers, was followed by a blessing.
This gives an insight into the kind of woman Naomi was.

''May the Lord deal kindly with you as you have dealt with the
dead and with me'' (1:8). Naomi added a blessing that the Lord
grant the women rest ''in the house of her husband,'' suggesting
they remarry. Naomi kissed the two women. They all wept.

At first, neither girl wanted to leave Naomi, proving that she
was a special kind of mother-in-law. They wanted to return to her
people, but Naomi reasoned against this.

She was too old to bear sons who could grow up to marry
Orpah and Ruth. Even if she were to have a husband that very
night, the girls wouldn't wait. They'd not refrain from remarrying
before then. No, Naomi insisted, it was harder for her than for the
younger women. ''For the hand of the Lord has gone forth against
me,'' Naomi concluded (Ruth 1:13).

Naomi does not curse God for her misfortune. Her statement
was, as later expressed, an admission that the Lord gives and the
Lord takes away; ''blessed be the name of the Lord.''

They wept again, Orpah kissed Naomi good-bye, and the older
woman turned her concern to Ruth. ''Your sister-in-law has gone
back to her people, and her gods; return after your sister-in-law''
(Ruth 1:15).

Naomi's ears then heard those incredibly moving words from

Ruth: "Do not urge me to leave you or turn back from following you; for where you go, I will go, and where you lodge, I will lodge. Your people shall be my people, and your God, my God" (1:16).

Naomi's God appealed to the Moabitess more than the fertility deities of her own people. Perhaps most of that had been learned from the way Naomi lived with her God, even in the loss of husband and sons.

Naomi also heard Ruth declare, "Where you die, I will die, and there I will be buried. Thus may the Lord do to me, and worse, if anything but death parts you and me" (1:17).

Naomi, seeing Ruth's tremendous sincerity and undoubtedly moved by the force of such a commitment, said no more. The two women went to Jerusalem.

The whole city was stirred. We see something of the city women's reaction to their long-absent woman friend. "Is this Naomi?"

She replied, "Do not call me Naomi (Pleasant) but Mara (Bitter), for the Almighty has dealt very bitterly with me." She had gone out full, but the Lord had brought her back empty. "Why do you call me Naomi, since the Lord has witnessed against me, and the Almighty has afflicted me?" (1:21).

Naomi was bitter because of what had happened through the Lord's afflictions. But she was not saying things against God; she was simply saying what she thought.

The people apparently didn't heed her name-change suggestion, for she was still called Naomi after that.

The Bible recounts how Ruth and Naomi reached Bethlehem at the start of the barley season. This was probably late March or early April, since planting was in October when the rains began. In the high country of Judea, a good six months was needed for the food grain to reach maturity.

Ruth asked Naomi for permission to go in and glean after the harvesters. The suggestion is that Ruth was a proper young woman and politely sought authority from her mother-in-law. Naomi agreed, and Ruth went out to do some hard work.

There was an ancient injunction from the Lord to Moses which explains what Naomi's daughter-in-law went to do. "Now when you reap the harvest of your land, you shall not reap to the very corners of your field, neither shall you gather the gleanings of your harvest.

"Nor shall you glean your vineyard, nor shall you gather the fallen fruit of your vineyard; you shall leave them for the needy and for the stranger" (Lev. 19:10-11).

The young widow went to a field that belonged to Boaz, who was from the same family as Naomi's late husband. Naomi didn't learn where Ruth had gleaned until that evening when the daughter-in-law returned with plenty of barley. That food, incidentally, was primarily for livestock. City residents preferred the better wheat. But food was food, and widows had no great choice.

Naomi was in the city when her daughter-in-law returned that evening with the barley. Naomi inquired where Ruth had gleaned, adding a blessing on the man who had allowed her to pick up the leftovers in his field (Ruth 2:19).

Ruth identified their benefactor as a man named Boaz. Naomi again blessed him and identified him as a close relative. Naomi's thoughts are not given, but she obviously thought of something very important about this time: the cultural rights of relatives. Naomi instructed Ruth in what to do.

First, she was to stay close to Boaz's maids "lest others fall upon you in another field" (2:22). This could have referred to other women gleaners being less charitable than Boaz's maids. It could also mean that a young widow might be victimized by unscrupulous men if she strayed far from Boaz's maids.

Next, Naomi instructed her daughter-in-law about a Hebrew custom involving a relative's protection. The young widow agreed to follow Naomi's instructions.

The Scriptures switch from Naomi's viewpoint to Ruth's and Boaz's, omitting the older widow's activities until Boaz and Ruth married. The Bible resumes Naomi's narrative when Ruth bears Boaz a son. The townswomen wished Naomi well, blessed the Lord and the child, and concluded with a hope. "May he also be to you a restorer of life and a sustainer of your old age; for your daughter-in-law, who loves you and is better to you than seven sons, has given birth to him" (4:15).

Naomi became the child's nurse, but the townswomen saw the relationship as being much closer than that. They said, "A son has been born to Naomi!"

The child was named Obed. He was King David's grandfather and became part of the genealogy of Jesus the Christ.

The Scriptures close Naomi's chronicle by showing her with the infant on her lap and the townswomen hailing her as a mother. She was fulfilled again.

The story is relevant today because it shows the human emotions of a woman who lost all she had, was thrice bereaved, and yet stayed true to God. Through the unlikely medium of a foreign daughter-in-law, Naomi found happiness again. And out of Naomi's story has come some of the most stirring words of faithfulness in all the Old Testament.

Naomi helped Ruth without complaint, was deeply loved in return, and jointly had her struggles of widowhood and poverty turned to joy. Naomi lived to bounce a child on her lap again and so held the link from Judah to David to Christ. Could any woman have asked more?

RACHEL

REFERENCES: Genesis 29:6-31; 30:1-8, 14-15, 22-25; 31:14-19, 33-35; 33:1-7; 35:16-20, 24; 46:19, 22; Ruth 4:11; 1 Samuel 10:2; Jeremiah 31:5; Matthew 2:18

SCRIPTURAL SYNOPSIS:

Rachel was the beautiful younger daughter of Laban the Syrian. She and her older sister, Leah, were given in marriage by their father to Jacob. Each of the sisters also gave her handmaiden to their husband.

Rachel was bitter because she was childless, while her sister and the two maids all produced offspring for Jacob. Eventually, Rachel had a son, Joseph. She died in the birth of her second son, Benjamin. Along with her sister, Rachel is credited in Scripture with building the house of Israel.

COMMENTARY:

This is the classical tale of a beautiful younger sister with a less-attractive sibling who vie for the love of the same man. But in this case, Rachel had the love of their shared husband, but was childless. Her less-loved sister, however, had six sons and a daughter.

The Scriptures open in Paddan-aram, an area north of where the Euphrates and Khabur rivers converge near the top of the Fertile Crescent.

Rachel, a young woman of unspecified age, but beautiful of form and figure, has come to a well in a field. It was the custom for shepherds to gather their sheep at the well and wait until all had arrived before removing the stone and watering every flock at once.

As the lovely shepherdess approached the well, she saw a stranger talking to the shepherds who had preceded her. The young man was Jacob, a fugitive from the vengeful wrath of his twin brother, Esau, whom Jacob had cheated out of a birthright.

Rachel didn't know it, but the stranger had been asking the shepherds about her father, Laban. Rachel didn't have to wait for the other sheep to arrive, for the stranger rolled the stone from the well's mouth and watered Rachel's sheep. Then she was kissed by the stranger, who wept as he explained who he was.

Rachel was Jacob's cousin. Her father, Laban, was a brother to Jacob's mother, Rebekah, who had married Isaac, son of the Hebrew patriarch Abraham, and moved to Canaan. There she had borne twins, Esau and Jacob. Rebekah and Isaac had sent Jacob to the land where Abraham had lived. The Scriptures do not tell us whether or not Jacob revealed his cheating past or told Rachel that he was a fugitive from his brother's sworn intention to kill him.

Rachel ran to tell her father that his mother's son had arrived. Laban greeted Jacob, his nephew, warmly and invited him to stay.

After a month, Rachel's father asked Jacob what he'd like for wages to work for him. Jacob already had fallen in love with Rachel. He agreed to serve her father seven years in exchange for Rachel in marriage. The agreement was made, but Laban was even more deceitful than Jacob had been with Esau.

The bride's father made a feast to celebrate the wedding. Then Laban switched brides.

There is no indication of how Rachel felt when the man who

loved her ended up the day after his wedding with her less-attractive sister, Leah. Rachel must have been pleased, however, when her cousin angrily faced his new father-in-law with the charges of fraud.

Laban was apparently not disturbed. He told his nephew that it was customary for the older sister to be married before the younger. In the seven years Jacob had served Laban, it seems someone would have explained the custom to Jacob; perhaps Rachel's own interests would have dictated she make that clear. The fact that she did not suggests that perhaps her father was lying and that he simply wanted to unload a daughter he knew he would have trouble marrying off.

The results were predictable. Leah's father agreed to give Rachel to Jacob if he would complete the bridal week with Leah and serve another seven years. Jacob was so much in love with Rachel that he ended up serving another seven years for her.

But conflicts were inevitable, too. Jacob loved Rachel the beautiful, but her sister was unloved. So God gave Leah four sons in a row while Rachel remained barren.

Rachel was jealous of her fruitful sister. Rachel spoke heartsick words to her husband. "Give me children, or else I die" (Gen. 30:1).

Jacob was angry. "Am I in the place of God, who has withheld from you the fruit of the womb?" (Gen. 30:2).

Rachel gave her maid, Bilhah, so that she could "bear on my knees, that through her I too may have children" (30:3).

This was an acceptable practice, with the resulting children being counted as the wife's through her maid. Bilhah bore two sons for Rachel. After the birth of the second son, Naphtali, Rachel revealed just how much she resented her sister. "With mighty wrestlings I have wrestled with my sister, and I have indeed prevailed" (Gen. 30:8).

To this point, Rachel has demonstrated unpleasant human emotions, jealousy and resentment. She had her husband's love, but she was unfulfilled. Apparently she was desperate for children, for she bargained with her sister for some mandrakes which Leah's son had found.

Mandrakes are rare plants that produce a yellow fruit resembling a small tomato. It was regarded as an aphrodisiac, although there is no scientific basis for the supposition. But Rachel apparently was convinced the plant could be used as a love potion. She had a squabble with her sister, with Leah crying out bitterly.

"Is it a small matter for you to take my husband? And would you take my son's mandrakes also?" (Gen. 30:15).

Rachel's power over Jacob was demonstrated in her reply. "Therefore he may lie with you tonight in return for your son's mandrakes" (30:16).

Ironically, Leah again became pregnant and presented her husband with a fifth son. Then she had a sixth son and a daughter — but Rachel remained childless.

Then, and only then, did Rachel finally become pregnant. She said, "God has taken away my reproach," and named the boy Joseph with the thought that the Lord might give her another son (30:23-24).

After the birth of her first child, Rachel with her sister and their maids, the various children, and the one husband planned to leave and go to Jacob's home. He had completed the fourteen years of service.

Laban, Rachel's father, persuaded Jacob to stay on. In the next six years, Laban switched his son-in-law's wages ten times, but God was with Jacob. He ended up wealthy, with large flocks, male and female servants, camels and donkeys. But Rachel's unnamed brothers turned their father against Jacob, claiming he had taken away "all that was our father's" (31:1).

Under God's instructions, Jacob left for his home without telling Rachel's father or brothers. Rachel and Leah seemed to have at least softened their tensions by this time, for both agreed to go with Jacob.

However, Rachel stole some of her father's household idols. This action suggests that Rachel had not yet accepted her husband's God. She was still holding on to her ancestral deities. The action led to a search by her father, who caught up with the fugitives.

When Laban searched her tent, Rachel pleaded that she could

not rise from the camel's saddle where she was seated. "Let not my lord be angry that I cannot rise before you, for the manner of women is upon me" (31:35).

Actually, she was lying. She had hidden the idols in the saddle. But her father didn't find them, and he and Jacob parted amicably.

There is little in this woman to make her likable or admirable. Yet her husband showed his preference for her over her sister when they continued on and word came that Esau was coming with four hundred men.

It had been twenty years since Jacob had defrauded his brother and fled his wrath. Jacob feared the approach of his twin, for such a large body of men meant Esau planned to attack.

While Jacob sent gifts in hopes of appeasing his brother, Rachel and her son were placed in the last of four companies. The two maids and their sons were ahead, followed by Leah and her family, with Rachel and Joseph in the rear, and safest, position.

During this critical period, God changed Jacob's name from Jacob (Grabber, or One Who Takes By the Heel or Surplants) to Israel. The name change came after Jacob wrestled with "a man" (Gen. 32:24) who declared, "Your name shall no longer be Jacob, but Israel; for you have striven with God and with men and have prevailed" (Gen. 32:28). Hosea (12:4) declares Jacob took his brother by the heel in the womb but "in his maturity he contended with God. Yes, he wrestled with the angel and prevailed." The name change is seen as spiritual progress Jacob/Israel had made.

Nothing is said about Rachel's attitude. We do not know that she ever really changed. However, there is a strong indication she did not make some spiritual adjustments after Esau arrived and a peaceful meeting was held that reunited the twin brothers.

For a while after that, the family settled in Shechem, in Canaan. Jacob ordered his household and all others with him to "put away the foreign gods which are among you, and purify yourselves" (35:2).

The Scriptures say, "So they gave to Jacob all the foreign gods which they had," without specifying exactly who was involved. But the logical assumption is that Rachel surrendered her father's stolen images.

This seems to be a highly critical spot in the narrative about Rachel, although it is not as clear as could be wished. However, consider the single remaining incident involving this beautiful woman and the high regard with which she was held thereafter.

As the people neared Ephrath (Bethlehem) after leaving Bethel, Rachel had hard labor with her second child. The mother called him Ben-oni, meaning the son of my sorrow. But Jacob called the child Benjamin, or "the son of my right hand."

Rachel died and was buried on the way to Bethlehem. Her story is ended at that point, but the honor given her in Ruth 4:11 suggests knowledge not available to us. "May the Lord make the woman who is coming into your home," well-wishers said to Boaz of Ruth, "like Rachel and Leah, both of whom built the house of Israel" (Ruth 4:11).

Rachel, like her husband in the early part of his life, was not a model of righteousness. Rachel was beautiful and loved by her husband, but for years she was jealous of her sister's fruitful womb. Rachel sold her husband's connubial rights to her sister for some mandrake roots. Because of her desperate yearning to be fulfilled as a mother, Rachel was willing to rely upon a superstition about the mandrake's power to help her conceive a child.

She argued with her husband about her inability to conceive and sparked his own angry retort.

Rachel stole her father's idols. She lied to him. She deceived her husband, who did not know she had the images hidden in her belongings.

Ultimately, this very human person, with all the emotions and feelings of a less-desirable nature, became honored because her two sons were founders of two of the twelve tribes of Israel. Rachel's name is listed before her sister's in this reference, although Leah was the older sister and first married to Jacob.

The Scriptures hold Rachel up as a paragon of motherhood who helped build a great nation of people. There can be no doubt that in her story there is something that made her worthy of such high regard.

It's difficult to understand why such an incident as the mandrake bargaining is included in the Bible while a clearer picture of

Rachel's later life is omitted. Yet perhaps it is not really omitted, but is implied in the surrendering of the images near Shechem.

Perhaps, like her husband, whose encounters with the God of his father, Isaac, and grandfather, Abraham, are detailed, Rachel also met Almighty God, and her life was changed for the better. The human feeling and behavior of Rachel are still very real today in the hearts and lives of many women. And, to them, like Rachel, the Scriptures hold out hope that they will be remembered as helping build God's house here on earth.

REBEKAH/REBECCA
REFERENCES: Genesis 22:23; 25:20-28; 26:7-11, 35; 27:1-46; 28:1-7; 29:12-13; 35:8; 49:31; Romans 9:10-12
SCRIPTURAL SYNOPSIS:

Young and beautiful Rebekah came to draw water from a spring near her parents' home in Haran, a city in Aram-naharaim (Paddan-aram) in Mesopotamia. There she saw a man-servant with some camels. The man had prayed for a test that Rebekah met. He revealed his mission to her father, Bethuel, a Syrian, son of Milcah and Nahor. Abraham, a relative of Bethuel's, wanted a bride for his son, Isaac, of his own people. Rebekah agreed to go with Abraham's servant and marry, sight-unseen, the forty-year-old Isaac.

After a long period of barrenness, Isaac prayed and God allowed Rebekah to conceive twins. They struggled in her womb, so she inquired of the Lord. He told her that two nations were in her womb. The older child would serve the younger, and the people from one child would be stronger than the other.

Esau was born first. He was a hairy man. His brother, Jacob, was born holding onto his twin's heel.

Isaac loved the first-born son, who was a hunter. Rebekah loved the quieter Jacob.

A famine drove Isaac and Rebekah to Gerar, an inland town near the border of Egypt and Palestine. King Abimelech of the Philistines and other men there were deceived by Isaac into thinking the beautiful Rebekah was his sister. Isaac had feared for his life if the Philistines knew Rebekah was his wife, so he had devised the deception. But when Abimelech saw Isaac caressing Rebekah, the king guessed the truth. He ordered his people not to touch Rebekah.

Isaac became very wealthy in Gerar. When he was old and nearly blind, he called his first-born son to him in order to discuss the blessing and the inheritance Esau would receive. Esau was instructed to hunt game, make Isaac's favorite dish, and when the old man had eaten, he would bless his first-born.

Rebekah overheard this and called Jacob. She conspired with him to trick Isaac into blessing the younger son while he thought he was blessing Esau. Esau had alienated himself from his mother's favor when he had married two Hittite women, women who did not know the God of Isaac.

The ruse worked. But Esau was so angry he'd lost his blessing that he swore to kill Jacob when their father was dead.

Rebekah learned of the danger. She convinced her husband to send Jacob to Paddan-aram and take a bride from the house of Bethuel (Rebekah's father), specifically, from among his cousins, the daughters of Laban, Rebekah's brother (Gen. 27:43; 28:2). Rebekah told Isaac she didn't want their son to take a bride from "the daughters of Heth" (Hittites). But Rebekah told Jacob a different story: he was to stay with her brother, Laban, until Esau's anger subsided. It would probably be only a few days; then she'd send for Jacob. "Why should I be bereaved of you both in one day?" Rebekah concluded (Gen. 27:45).

While Jacob was gone, Esau took a wife of the descendants of Ishmael, who was Isaac's half-brother. The marriage into Abraham's line was to ease the pain and displeasure Esau had caused his mother and father by marrying Hittites.

Rebekah's favorite son was well received in Haran when Jacob mentioned his relationship as nephew to Laban, Rebekah's brother.

Rebekah was apparently dead before Jacob returned twenty years later married to Leah and Rachel, Laban's daughters. Rebekah was buried in Hebron in the same family cave with Isaac's parents, Abraham and Sarah.

The New Testament mentions Rebekah's twins in connection with God's pre-ordained purpose that the older (Esau) would serve the younger (Jacob) because God hated Esau and loved Jacob. Paul the apostle uses Rebekah's sons as an example of the "children of the promise" — children who through Abraham were spiritual descendants of Jesus Christ.

COMMENTARY:

To understand Rebekah's importance in Scripture, it is necessary to place her in proper perspective from Abraham's time.

Abraham, the greatest and first patriarch, had a son by Sarah. The son was Isaac, who had been promised by God years before. Through this son all the earth was to be blessed. The land of Canaan was also to be given to Abraham's descendants.

When Sarah and Abraham were very old, the patriarch called his most trusted (but nameless) servant and instructed him to go to Haran, where Abraham had stopped a while on his trip up from Ur on his way to Canaan. The servant was to swear by "the God of heaven and the God of earth" to take a wife for Isaac from among Abraham's relatives. Abraham did not want his son to marry one of the pagan Canaanites.

The servant obeyed. He led a ten-camel caravan to Haran and waited outside the city by a well. The servant prayed to Abraham's God, asking Him to confirm the right wife for Isaac through specific signs.

At evening, when the women came to draw water, Rebekah came to the well with a pitcher on her shoulder. She was very beautiful, a virgin, a daughter of Bethuel, the son of Milcah, wife of Abraham's brother Nahor. She was a sister of Laban, who was a Syrian.

The Scriptures are clear that Rebekah was divinely chosen by God to be the wife of Abraham's son, Isaac. Rebekah was to be the second matriarch, following Sarah, in producing the man (Jacob/Israel) who was to sire the twelve sons (tribes) of Israel. One of these (Judah, Rebekah's grandson) was to be a direct ancestor of Jesus through Joseph of Galilee.

It is interesting to note how Rebekah viewed her role and how her personality changed as time went on.

When we meet Rebekah in Scripture, she is young, virginal,

thoughtful, kind, and considerate. Unknown to her, the unnamed servant whom she met at the well had just prayed to his master's (Abraham's) God for the right wife for Isaac to be revealed by doing certain things.

The lovely Rebekah met the first condition by drawing water for the traveling servant. Then she volunteered to draw water for his ten camels. That was no small chore, but it confirmed the servant's prayer. Satisfied that God had answered him, the servant produced a gold ring and bracelets. Then he asked, ''Whose daughter are you? Please tell me, is there room for us to lodge in your father's house?'' (Gen. 24:23).

The girl identified herself as Bethuel's daughter and said there was hospitality available at her father's house.

At this information, the nameless servant bowed to worship God. He had guided the servant to ''the house of my master's brothers'' (Gen. 24:27).

Rebekah ran to tell her family, including her brother, Laban. He was something of a scoundrel, as later developments show. But in that moment he was the perfect host, perhaps because he was impressed by the new gold jewelry his sister exhibited. In view of Rebekah's later deceitfulness, it may be assumed she learned some of that from Laban.

The Scriptures detail how Abraham's unnamed servant stated his mission. He told how he had prayed and Rebekah had met the conditions of the petition.

Laban and his father, Bethuel, both agreed the matter was from the Lord. Rebekah was free to go marry Isaac. The servant wanted to leave the next day, but Laban's and Rebekah's mother naturally wanted the girl to stay with them a few days longer. The decision was left up to Rebekah.

''I will go,'' she said (24:58).

There was something unusual in allowing a woman, especially as young as Rebekah, to make her own decision in a male-dominated society. But she did not mince words. She went with a brief, positive statement to marry a man she'd never met, a long way from her family home, and in a strange country where strange gods were worshiped.

The uniqueness of Rebekah's personality is next displayed when she and the servant reached the Negev, south of what later became Palestine. When the servant identified Isaac as he walked toward them from the field, Rebekah took a veil or shawl and covered herself.

There was no mention of a courtship. The Scriptures simply say Isaac brought Rebekah to his mother's tent, where Rebekah became his wife and "Isaac was comforted after his mother's death" (Gen. 24:67).

Rebekah was barren for some time following her marriage.

There is no mention of what Rebekah thought when she learned that Abraham had another son, Ishmael, by Hagar, the Egyptian who had been Sarah's maid.

We know that Rebekah became the wife of a man who was promised of God to become a father of nations. Surely Abraham told his daughter-in-law about God's promises to him through Isaac. Yet the Scriptures are mute on this part of Rebekah's life.

The years of barrenness that Sarah had suffered before Isaac was born are not apparently comparable to Rebekah's. But we can't help wondering how Rebekah felt when she knew that God had promised so much, and yet she was childless. She asked her husband to intervene with God on her behalf. She became pregnant.

The new life within caused her some concern, for there was a struggle in the womb. This time, Rebekah did not ask her husband to pray for her. She "went to inquire of the Lord" about the struggle within her body (25:22).

God told her that two nations were in her womb. Two peoples would be separated from her body; one people would be stronger than the other. "And the older shall serve the younger" (25:23).

The Bible writers do not give any hint of how Rebekah reacted to such news. Perhaps the significance of God's words was lost to her in the joy of knowing she was to finally not only have a child, but twins. It remained for Paul the apostle to point out the tremendous importance of this godly announcement (Rom. 9:10-11).

Rebekah bore Esau first. He was red and hairy, a description made at birth, with emphasis on the fact he was like a hairy garment (Gen 25:25).

The twin followed closely at the birth, coming into the world with his hand on the heel of his brother, Esau. Jacob was named for his first act in the world, with his name being translated as "Grabber," one who takes by the heel, or one who supplants. The meaning is significant in light of both the message God had given Rebekah and what later happened.

Isaac was then sixty, so Rebekah had been barren about nineteen years (25:26).

The first hint of Rebekah's character change comes in the scriptural declaration that Isaac loved Esau but Rebekah loved Jacob. The twins grew up to be quite unlike each other, with Esau a skillful hunter and a man of the field, while Jacob was peaceful, dwelling in tents.

There is no hint of parental involvement in the famous episode of Esau's selling his birthright to Jacob for some stew. The red-colored dish was traded for the right of the first-born son, and Esau received a new name: Edom.

There is a hint of how beautiful Rebekah remained in her mature years when the Scriptures next tell about the famine which drove Isaac and his wife to Gerar. By then the twins were grown. Even assuming they were as young as twenty, plus the twenty years Rebekah had spent as a wife before bearing the twins, she had to have been at least in her middle fifties.

Yet her husband had been afraid the Philistines would kill him for Rebekah, so he had lied and said she was his sister. Some researchers question this story as being too much like the same kind of event that caused Abraham to lie about Sarah's relationship to him. However, the Scriptures tell the story, and so we accept it for what it declares. That includes the statement that Rebekah was still beautiful.

Isaac caressed his wife one day when King Abimelech of the Philistines saw them. There was an edge in the king's words which implied that one of the Philistines might have had sexual relations with Rebekah and brought guilt upon them. This poses the question of whether it was simply a statement made by an upset king, or whether Rebekah would not have had any rights in denying the desires of a Philistine wanting her for personal pleasure. It is one of those ancient cultural situations which cannot be satisfactorily resolved.

The incident also leaves unanswered the part that Rebekah played in the deceit fostered upon the men among whom she and her husband lived. However, it is clear that the culture saw a guilt associated with sleeping with another man's wife. At the same time, there is a suggestion that no such guilt would have resulted if the woman was an eligible sister of the Hebrew man in their midst.

Except for one terse sentence, Scripture is silent regarding Rebekah's emotions when her first-born son married: "And when Esau was forty years old he married Judith the daughter of Beeri the Hittite and Basemath the daughter of Elon the Hittite; and they brought grief to Isaac and Rebekah" (26:34-35).

It may have been this which prompted Rebekah to become a conspirator against her first-born twin and against her husband. The Scriptures do not make it clear, but the next event recorded after this marriage to pagan women is the one in which Rebekah became deceitful.

She overheard her aged and nearly blind husband tell Esau to go into the field, shoot game, prepare a savory dish, and receive the blessing as the right of the first-born son.

Rebekah called her favorite son, Jacob, explained what she had heard, and instructed him in a plan to circumvent her husband's intended blessing. Jacob pointed out the hazards involved with trying to fool his father when Esau was hairy and Jacob was a smooth man. Jacob might get a curse instead of a blessing.

Rebekah replied, "Your curse be on me, my son; only obey my voice" (27:13).

This is a totally different woman from the virgin whom Abraham's servant had found. Rebekah's motives are not explained, although she loved Jacob, and perhaps Esau's Canaanite wives and his action in taking them had offended her. It has also been suggested that Rebekah remembered what God said about the older serving the younger, and she was trying to hurry that prophecy along. Yet there is nothing in Scripture to suggest God needs deceit to carry out His plans.

Whatever her reasoning, Rebekah successfully carried out the deception. She was so determined to do this that she was willing to take upon her own head any curse which might follow. She was able to persuade her favorite son to act with her in the conspiracy.

It might help to know if she was aware that Esau had sold his birthright to his twin, but the Scriptures don't say, and we can only conclude that Rebekah was adamant about succeeding in her designs.

She went to some lengths to fool her husband, putting Esau's best clothes on Jacob and placing the skins of goat kids on Jacob's hands and neck to make him feel like his hairy brother. She also made the kind of food her husband loved and then waited for the outcome.

Isaac fell for the deception. Jacob, dressed as his brother and with the food, persuaded his father that it was Esau who stood before his blind eyes. Jacob lied and succeeded in stealing the blessing of his father.

When Esau arrived and discovered the trick, it was too late for him to receive the blessing originally intended. Jacob had been made master of his older brother. Jacob had been blessed with grain and new wine. But when Esau wept, his father gave him an alternate blessing.

Esau was to live by his sword. He was to serve his brother, but eventually the yoke would be broken off his neck.

Rebekah may have consoled herself that this blessing was exactly what God had told her to expect when the twins struggled within her womb. But the Scriptures do not say what she thought or felt. The next mention of her is when word is brought to her that the angry, frustrated Esau plans to kill Jacob. But Esau will wait until his father is dead.

Rebekah faced the prospects of a double loss, the death of her aged husband and the murdering of one son by another. No matter how she looked at it, Rebekah was about to become a widow with extra grief from a murdering son and a dead son.

Yet nothing is said of Rebekah's thoughts. She simply acted. In the first act, she was honest. She told Jacob to flee for safety to Haran and her brother, Laban. When Esau's wrath had subsided, she would send for Jacob to come home.

In the second action, Rebekah lied to her husband and concealed her motives in sending Jacob away. She told her husband she was "tired of living because of the daughters of Heath," a reference to her two Canaanite daughters-in-law whom Esau had married.

Rebekah added, "If Jacob takes a wife from the daughters of Heth, like these, from the daughters of the land, what good will my life be to me?" (27:46).

Isaac responded to his wife's rationale. He called in Jacob, blessed him, and charged him not to marry a Canaanite. Instead, he was to go to Paddan-aram, to Bethuel, "your mother's father; and from there take to yourself a wife from the daughters of Laban, your mother's brother" (28:2).

Isaac included a blessing upon the son who had deceived him, concluding, "May He also give you the blessings of Abraham, to you and to your descendants with you; that you may possess the land of your sojournings, which God gave to Abraham" (28:4).

Rebekah's duplicity had saved her favorite son's life. Rebekah's husband had given to Jacob the blessings which had been promised to his grandfather, Abraham: possession of Canaan, the Promised Land.

Jacob's flight was seen by his twin brother as obedience to their mother and father. The realization of how strongly the parents felt about a "proper" wife caused Esau to take a third bride, Mahalath, Ishmael's daughter, or a direct descendant of Abraham.

The final Old Testament mention of Rebekah shows she was buried in the patriarch's tomb at Hebron with Abraham, Sarah, Isaac, and Leah, first of Jacob's wives.

Thus Rebekah reposed with the founding fathers and mother of the Hebrews, who later became the Jews, and eventually possessed the Promised Land and became numerous as the sands of the sea, as God had promised Abraham.

Rebekah's story is a strangely disturbing one. She began life as a sterling example of womanhood, then is left with a shadow of dishonesty, unfairness, lying, and other unpleasant human attributes. The fact that she was buried in such distinguished company suggests she may have completed her life on a more positive note than where the Scriptures leave her in the last dramatic episode.

She apparently never saw her favorite son again after he fled his revengeful brother. We can only assume that this separation in her declining years may have contributed to some good changes which are not specified in the Old Testament.

But the last full glimpse of Rebekah in Genesis is distressing, which may be why Paul the apostle gives us a cameo summation in Romans. There we see that God's sovereignty was evident in Rebekah's life, and that she was an instrument of God's plans. Whether her human traits were all good or not doesn't seem to have been an issue in making Rebekah a part of something much greater than she could have dreamed.

Paul's letter to the Romans is explaining the issue of God's plans and purposes, and His characteristic of determining what shall be done in His sovereignty.

Rebekah had conceived twins by "our father Isaac," Paul declares. Before the twins were born "and had not done anything good or bad, in order that God's purpose according to His choice might stand, not because of works, but because of Him who calls, it was said of her, 'The older will serve the younger.' Just as it is written, 'Jacob I loved, but Esau I hated'" (Rom. 9:10-13).

Paul's conclusion to his statements involving Rebekah challenges the human supposition that such things make God unjust (Rom. 9:20-21). Instead, Paul explains, the Potter has the right over the clay to make of each lump what He wants, and for noble or common uses.

Rebekah, then, remains a study in a woman who began her scriptural appearance as one kind of person and left with less desirable characteristics. Yet in the end she rested with the mothers and fathers of the founding dynasty of the Hebrews/Jews, and God's sovereignty accomplished His purpose for mankind.

It is a deep study in both theology and human behavior, but Rebekah is still there for us to learn from after some thirty-seven hundred years.

RUTH
REFERENCES: book of Ruth and Matthew 1:5
SCRIPTURAL SYNOPSIS:

Ruth was a Moabitess who married Mahlon, son of Elimelech and Naomi, Bethlehemites who had spent about ten years in Moab because of a famine in Judah. Ruth's husband died, as did Naomi's husband plus Chilion, Ruth's brother-in-law.

Ruth refused to leave Naomi and accepted her God and her people. The two widows journeyed to Bethlehem, where Ruth met Boaz while gleaning in his fields. Through Naomi's guidance, Ruth married Boaz. They had a son, Obed, who became grandfather to King David. Ruth thus became part of the genealogy from Judah to Jesus.

COMMENTARY:

Sometime during the ten years that the Ephrathites from Bethlehem in Judea lived in Moab, Ruth met and married Mahlon. It was seemingly not a good match. The Moabites were of low spiritual status compared to the Hebrews. Moabites worshiped fertility deities and were constantly criticized by the Hebrew prophets. Yet this Moabite woman became part of a God-fearing family.

Ruth became a widow while still childless. So did her sister-in-law, Orpah, who had married Mahlon's brother, Chilion. Their father-in-law also died. The loss of father and two sons is speculated to have perhaps been the result of an epidemic.

Ruth and her sister-in-law apparently started with Naomi for Bethlehem when the famine ended in Judea. But Orpah turned back. Ruth, however, declined her mother-in-law's suggestion to return to Moab.

In making her decision to cast her lot with Naomi, Ruth spoke some of the most enduring words in the world: "Do not urge me to leave you or turn back from following you; for where you go, I will go, and where you lodge, I will lodge. Your people shall be my people, and your God, my God.

"Where you die, I will die, and there will I be buried. Thus may the Lord do to me, and worse, if anything but death parts you and me" (1:16-17).

The two widows arrived in the Hebrew woman's homeland at

the beginning of barley harvest. This crop was planted about October, "in the latter rains," and harvested in late March or early April in the Judean highlands. The harvest normally lasted from Passover to Pentecost.

The Scriptures give us an example of how widows survived in the time of Ruth. She asked her mother-in-law for permission to glean in a field where she could "find favor." The requirement for farmers to leave something from the harvest for the needy and strangers was given by God to Moses (Lev. 19:10-11).

Naomi gave Ruth permission. She went to a field and approached the reapers. "Please let me glean and gather after the reapers among the sheaves," she said (2:7). Again, permission was granted by the servant in charge.

Ruth worked all morning gathering up the barley that the reapers missed. It was hard, backbreaking work, for Ruth was picking up what was left. She had been sitting in a house for a little while when the owner of the field arrived from Bethlehem.

He was Boaz, apparently an older man who noticed the young gleaner. The Scriptures do not make it clear if she overheard Boaz's inquiry about her, but his dialogue is recorded. The head reaper explained that she was the Moabitess who had returned with Naomi. She was a good worker, the servant had noticed.

Ruth was approached by Boaz. "Listen carefully, my daughter. Do not glean in another field; futhermore, do not go on from this one, but stay here with my maids" (2:8).

The man added that he had ordered his servants not to touch her. When they reaped in another field, she was to be allowed to glean after them there. When the girl got thirsty, she was to drink from what the servants had drawn from a well and put in jars.

Ruth fell on her face in the custom of her times and asked, "Why have I found favor in your sight that you should take notice of me, since I am a foreigner?" (2:10).

Boaz explained that he had fully learned what Ruth had done for her mother-in-law after her husband's death. Boaz had heard how Ruth had left her own father and mother and the land of her birth to come to a people previously unknown to her. Boaz concluded by saying, "May the Lord reward your work, and your wages be full from the Lord, the God of Israel, under whose wings you have come to seek refuge'' (2:12).

Ruth was grateful for her benefactor's kindness. This was extended at mealtime, when Boaz called her to share the bread and dip it in the vinegar. Boaz also gave her some roasted grain so she not only had enough to eat but even had some left over.

As Ruth arose to return to her work, Boaz ordered the reapers to allow her extra privileges.

When the evening came, Ruth beat out the barley from the chaff and had about an ephah. This was a dry measure roughly equal to about two-thirds of a bushel.

When Ruth returned home with food for Naomi, the older woman asked where Ruth had gleaned. When Ruth replied, Naomi blessed Boaz and explained he was a relative of her late husband, Elimelech.

Ruth told Naomi that Boaz had told her to stay close to his servants until the harvest was finished. The courtesy was extended into the wheat harvest. That was roughly the middle of April.

One day Naomi talked to Ruth about her desire to seek security for the young widow. The Scriptures do not detail Naomi's thinking, or what Ruth thought, but the older woman had obviously made up her mind to do something specific under Hebrew custom. It had to be done while Boaz was winnowing barley that very night.

Ruth listened as Naomi told her what to do.

''Wash yourself therefore, and anoint yourself and put on your best clothes, and go down to the threshing floor; but do not make yourself known to the man until he has finished eating and drinking'' (3:3).

Ruth listened as Naomi completed her instructions. Then Ruth obeyed. She came to the threshing floor and waited for the sequence of events Naomi had said would happen.

When Boaz had eaten and drunk and his heart was merry, he went to the end of the grain heap and lay down. When he was asleep, Ruth quietly approached him, uncovered his feet, and lay down.

In the darkness of the night, Boaz awakened and realized a

woman was at his feet. He demanded, "Who are you?"

"I am Ruth your maid. So spread your covering over your maid, for you are a close relative" (3:9).

The man realized the significance of Ruth's action. She was symbolically asking for his protection as a near male relative of her mother-in-law. He responded by declaring he would do whatever Ruth asked, "for all my people in the city know that you are a woman of excellence" (3:11).

However, Ruth learned, there was a closer relative who had the right of redemption ahead of Boaz. That relative would be offered the opportunity to redeem Ruth. If he failed, Boaz would do so.

The agreement made, Boaz had Ruth continue sleeping at his feet. But she arose before it was light enough for them to see each other. Boaz didn't want it known that a woman came to the threshing floor. He gave her six measures of barley in her cloak and she went into the city.

Ruth reported to Naomi and showed the gift Boaz had sent to Naomi. She assured Ruth that Boaz would not rest until he had settled the matter with the other relative.

Although Ruth undoubtedly was absent from the meeting of the principals who were to decide her future, the story gives a rich insight into the culture of the time.

Boaz sat in the city gate until the relative he sought came by. The man sat down at Boaz's invitation. Ten city men were also invited to join the group. They were to be witnesses to the transaction between Boaz and the nearer relative.

Naomi had to sell a piece of land that belonged to Elimelech, "our brother," Boaz explained. He was informing the man before the elders that if the nearer relative wanted to redeem the parcel, fine. If not, Boaz would do so, since he was next in line with that privilege.

The relative said he'd redeem the land.

Then Boaz sprang a surprise condition. "On the day you buy the field from the hand of Naomi, you must also acquire Ruth the Moabitess, the widow of the deceased, in order to raise up the name of the deceased on his inheritance" (4:5).

The nameless male relative backed down. He explained that it would jeopardize his own inheritance if he did that. So Boaz could exercise his right of redemption. In the custom of ancient Israel, the relative pulled off his sandal and handed it to Boaz.

Boaz called upon the elders to witness the formal agreement. Boaz had bought the land from Naomi which had been her husband's and sons'. And Boaz had also acquired Ruth to "raise up the name of the deceased on his inheritance, so that the name of the deceased may not be cut off from his brothers or from the court of his birthplace" (4:10).

The widow of the Hebrew, Mahlon, was to have an opportunity to have a child so Elimelech's inheritance would be passed on and Mahlon's name would not be "cut off."

The city elders agreed they had witnessed a legal transaction. They blessed Ruth and hoped she achieved fame and wealth in Ephrathah (Bethlehem). The blessing included a reference to Judah, of which Boaz was a direct descendant.

The Scriptures do not say how Ruth felt when she became the wife of Boaz, but she was an obedient woman, and the arranged marriage through Naomi seemed to please her. She bore Boaz a son, Obed. He became grandfather to the great king David, and Ruth, therefore, became not only David's ancestor but also a link to Joseph, husband of Mary, mother of Jesus.

Ruth was one of the biblical women of whom nothing unkind can be said. Her whole life testifies to her lovingkindness, first to her husband, then to her bereaved mother-in-law, and finally to a new husband and a son. Ruth had a choice of going back to the gods of her people or choosing Naomi's God. Ruth chose God.

Although she suffered the loss of a husband, Ruth was a woman of excellent character: loyal, kind, obedient, and loving. In time, God chose her to be an ancestor of David and Jesus and a sterling example of how one human lived above her circumstances.

TAMAR, who played the harlot
REFERENCES: Genesis 38:6, 11, 13-30; Ruth 4:12; 1
Chronicles 2:4
SCRIPTURAL SYNOPSIS:

The first Tamar mentioned in the Bible was twice married and
twice widowed, but she lived in hope of marrying again and
bearing a child. Finally, realizing she had been deceived, she
removed her widow's garments and pretended to be a harlot. She
became pregnant by her father-in-law, Judah. She bore twins. One
became an ancestor of Jesus.

COMMENTARY:

The story begins with Judah, one of the twelve sons born to
Jacob/Israel through his wives. Judah had saved his brother
Joseph's life when the other siblings wanted to kill the teenager.
Instead, with the older brother, Reuben, they had sold Joseph into
slavery. Their father grieved over the loss, and Judah left his
brothers to visit a certain Adullamite named Hirah.

There Judah saw a daughter of a Canaanite named Shua. She
bore Judah three sons: Er, Onan, and Shelah.

In the custom of the times, Judah chose a wife, Tamar, for Er,
his first-born. Tamar was widowed when Er, who was "evil in the
sight of the Lord," died because the Lord took his life (Gen.
38:7).

The levirate law given through Moses four hundred years later
naturally did not apply in Tamar's time, but details set down by
Moses in Deuteronomy 25:5-10 would have applied in Tamar's
case. If a brother died childless, the surviving brother was required
to marry the widow. The first-born child was to assume the name
of the dead brother so that his name "may not be blotted out from
Israel."

Judah ordered his second son, Onan, "Go in to your brother's
wife, and perform your duty as a brother-in-law to her, and raise
up offspring to your brother" (38:8).

Onan knew the offspring would not be his, so when "he went
in to his brother's wife, he wasted his seed on the ground, in order
not to give offspring to his brother" (38:9).

This displeased the Lord, who took Onan's life, too.

Judah said to his twice-widowed daughter-in-law, "Remain a widow in your father's house until my son Shelah grows up" (38:11).

But, the Bible explains, Judah was really afraid that the third and final son would also die.

Tamar went and lived in her father's house for a considerable time.

Judah's wife, Shua, died. When the time of mourning had ended, Judah the widower went up to his sheepshearers at Timnah, accompanied by his friend, Hirah the Addullamite. Addulam was a town southwest of Jerusalem.

Someone told Tamar, "Your father-in-law is going up to Timnah to shear his sheep" (38:13).

Tamar removed her widow's garments, covered herself with a veil, wrapped herself, and sat in the gateway of Enaim, which is on the road to Timnah. She did this because "she saw that Shelah had grown up, and she had not been given to him as a wife" (38:14).

When Judah saw Tamar, he didn't recognize her as his daughter-in-law because she had covered her face like a harlot.

Judah propositioned the woman. She asked, "What will you give me?" (38:16).

"I will send you a kid from the flock."

"Will you give a pledge until you send it?"

"What pledge shall I give you?" Judah asked.

"Your seal and your cord, and your staff that is in your hand" (38:18).

Judah agreed, surrendered the three items, and had sexual relations with Tamar.

Judah went on to shear sheep. Tamar left, removed her veil, and put back on her widow's garments.

Judah sent the promised kid from the flock by his friend, Hirah the Adullamite. Naturally, he couldn't find the woman. Hirah asked the men around the area, "Where is the temple prostitute who was by the road at Enaim?"

The local men replied, "There has been no temple prostitute here" (38:22).

Hirah returned to Judah and reported. Judah thought of his

pledge of seal, cord, and staff which he had been unable to redeem. Judah decided, "Let her keep them, lest we become a laughingstock. After all, I sent this kid, but you did not find her" (38:23).

Three months passed. Tamar was pregnant by her one encounter with her father-in-law. Word was brought to Judah.

"Your daughter-in-law Tamar has played the harlot, and behold, she is also with child by harlotry" (38:24).

Judah said, "Bring her out and let her be burned!"

As they were bringing Tamar out in obedience to her father-in-law's order, she sent a message to him. "I am with child by a man to whom these things belong. Please examine and see whose signet ring and cords and staff are these?" (38:25).

Judah recognized them. He said, "She is more righteous than I, inasmuch as I did not give her my son Shelah" (38:26).

She was permitted to live, although Judah didn't have relations with Tamar again.

Tamar bore twins. At their birth, one child put out a hand. The midwife tied a scarlet thread on that hand, saying, "This one came out first."

But the child withdrew his hand and his brother was born first. He was named Perez.

Then the brother with the scarlet thread was born. He was named Zerah (38:30).

The story ends there, with a couple of additional mentions for genealogical purposes. In 1 Chronicles 2:1-5, the line begins with Israel/Jacob, whose fourth-born son, Judah, had five sons, including Perez and Zerah, whom his daughter-in-law bore him. The genealogy carries through from Perez, the first-born twin, to David the king.

The Perezite branch of Judah's tribe is mentioned favorably in Ruth 4:12, when the witnesses blessed Boaz upon acquiring Ruth the Moabitess as his wife. The witnesses said, "Moreover, may your house be like the house of Perez whom Tamar bore to Judah, through the offspring which the Lord shall give you by this young woman."

In the New Testament, Matthew's genealogy begins with

Abraham and traces his descendants back through Isaac, Jacob, and Judah. Matthew adds, "And to Judah were born Perez and Zerah by Tamar" (Matt. 1:3). The genealogy is then traced to David and Solomon down until the line produced "Joseph the husband of Mary, by whom was born Jesus, who is called Christ" (Matt. 1:16).

The story of Tamar who played the harlot gives us a deeper insight into the customs of her times. Judah had three sons, two of whom were so evil in God's sight that He took their lives.

This great sin of Er, Judah's first-born son and Tamar's first husband, isn't given. But Er was the son of a Canaanite woman, Shua. The Canaanites had a fertility rite which was very lewd. These people had a pantheon of gods, including the highest male deity and his consort, Asherah. The other Canaanite gods included Baal, a name often used in the Bible as a symbol of idolatry. Perhaps it was his mother's religious background which made Er so evil that God killed him.

We know the sin of Judah's second-born son, Onan. He obeyed his Hebrew father by having sexual relations with his dead brother's widow, as Moses would someday formally require surviving brothers to do. But Onan didn't want a child to result from his union with Tamar because he didn't want to give his dead brother any heirs. The selfish Onan "wasted his seed on the ground." This displeased the Lord, and He took the offender's life.

Twice widowed, Tamar obeyed her father-in-law, went home to her father's house, and waited, in widow's clothing, for Judah's third son to grow up.

But Judah's motives were deceitful. He didn't give Tamar to the third and last surviving son, Shelah, even when he was grown.

Tamar tired of waiting to be a mother. She had been obedient and patient, and her father-in-law, now widowed, was obviously not going to give her to the third son. So Tamar took matters into her own hand.

She pretended to be a temple prostitute of the Canaanite religion. Tamar waited in her veil for Judah to come along. She was ready for his proposition. She wanted a pledge for her sexual favors — not actually as a guarantee that she would eventually receive a kid from the flock in payment — but for what she had obviously planned to do.

She conceived a child by her father-in-law, who ordered her burned when the pregnancy was made known to him. There was no stigma attached to the man's part in the relationship.

Tamar was calm. She said nothing until she was brought out for burning. She sent word to her father-in-law that she was pregnant by the man whose three pledges she then presented.

Judah admitted his daughter-in-law was more righteous than he. He had broken his word by not giving her to the third son as wife so she could have a child.

It was a man's prerogative to give a woman, even his daughter-in-law, to the son. This shows how little power the women of Tamar's day had. Tamar had to resort to trickery in order to make sure that Judah would in some way keep his word.

Afterward, Judah seems to have behaved in accordance with his self-appraisal that Tamar was more honorable than he. The later readings suggest he married her, but the Scriptures make it clear that he did not again have sexual relations with her. He apparently gave her what amounted to a "name only" relationship.

At the birth of twins, the midwife naturally identified the child who was apparently about to be born first. Even among twins, the right of the first-born was vital in Tamar's time. Yet the child with the scarlet thread around his arm was not born first. The other twin arrived instead, and the right of inheritance fell to him, called Perez, meaning "a breach."

The narrative leaves us with some unanswered questions. Did Tamar enjoy the right of true wife to her father-in-law? Did she want other children, or was she satisfied with the twins? Did she miss the continuing offices of a real husband? How was her illicit relationship with her deceitful father-in-law regarded by the community?

We can surmise some things about Tamar. She was a good woman, obedient to her father-in-law, trusting in his word and patiently wearing widow's clothing for years in her father's house. She apparently did not seek to fulfill her yearning for motherhood with other males in the area.

She waited until she saw she was deceived, and then she thoughtfully and carefully planned how — not to get revenge — but to achieve her rightful fulfillment as a mother of Judah's line.

Even when her pregnancy was known, and word was sent that she was to burn, she did not accuse her father-in-law to the people who were taking her to death.

Tamar must have had some very human thoughts as she waited to see what action Judah would take. He had ordered her burned as a Canaanite temple prostitute. He might have denied ownership of the pledges when she produced them. She might have feared her plan would fail and she would be condemned to die while Judah escaped punishment. But these do not seem to have been Tamar thoughts. She appears to have been sure of herself.

It seems Tamar was so astute a student of human nature that she knew her father-in-law would do the right thing and spare her life. But what a risk it seems now!

Tamar's story is often soft-peddled today because of the socially unacceptable fact of her incestuous relationship with her father-in-law. Yet the Bible makes it plain that everyone knew what happened.

There seems to be no biblical reproach for Tamar. She became the direct link from Abraham, Isaac, Jacob, and Judah to King David and Joseph, the husband of Mary, "by whom was born Jesus, who is called Christ."

It's a curious story, with an implication Tamar obviously could not have known in her lifetime. And yet, out of her womb came the fulfillment she sought as a mother, and a tie with God's promises which gave us Jesus Christ.

TAMAR, daughter of King David
REFERENCES: 2 Samuel 13:1-39; 1 Chronicles 3:9.
The second Tamar mentioned in the Bible
SCRIPTURAL SYNOPSIS:

Tamar was a beautiful young virgin princes daughter of King David. Absalom was her full brother, but Amnon was a half-brother. Amnon so lusted after Tamar that he made himself sick with frustration. A friend and cousin, Jonadab, shrewdly conspired with Amnon to gratify the prince's sexual desires with Tamar.

Amnon followed the deceitful plan, raped Tamar, and then threw her out. Tamar's brother, Absalom, bided his time and then avenged the rape by killing Amnon.

COMMENTARY:

Tamar, the second woman by that name in the Old Testament, is introduced when she was in the beauty of young maidenhood. She was a full sister to Absalom, David's third-born son. Tamar's and Absalom's mother was Maacah, princess daughter of Talmai, king of Geshur (1 Chron. 3:2).

Tamar, who lived about a thousand years before Jesus Christ was born, wore the traditional long-sleeved, varicolored tunic — confirming that she was a king's virgin daughter.

Her name is variously translated as "slender," "palm," or "palm tree." She was the granddaughter of a king and herself a princess through her father, the former shepherd boy who had become King David. He ruled over the combined monarchy of all twelve tribes in Israel.

Tamar's half-brother, Amnon, looked on her with such lust that he couldn't control himself.

Amnon was first-born of David's sons. His mother was Ahinoam the Jezreelitess (1 Chron. 3:1). Amnon's passion for his pretty half-sister was so great that he made himself ill. His friend, the shrewd Jonadab, a cousin (son of Shimeah, David's brother), asked Amnon why the king's son was so depressed each morning.

The prince replied, "I am in love with Tamar, the sister of my brother Absalom."

Amnon's cunning friend counseled, "Lie down on your bed and pretend to be ill; when your father comes to see you, say to him, 'Please let my sister Tamar come and give me some food to eat, and let her prepare the food in my sight, that I may see it and eat from her hand'" (2 Sam. 13:5).

Amnon obeyed. When the king came to see his son, Amnon asked to have Tamar come and make a couple of cakes while he watched, and he'd eat them from her hand.

David sent to the house for Tamar. "Go now to your brother Amnon's house, and prepare food for him" (13:7).

Tamar went to her half-brother's house. Amnon was lying down. She took dough, kneaded it, and made the cakes. When they were baked, Tamar took the pan and dished out the cakes to set before Amnon. But he refused to eat.

He said, "Have everyone go out from me" (13:9).

Everyone left. Tamar and Amnon were alone.

Amnon said to Tamar, "Bring the food into the bedroom, that I may eat from your hand" (13:10).

Tamar brought the cakes into Amnon's bedroom. But when she offered them to her half-brother, he took hold her her. "Come, lie with me, my sister" (13:11).

"No, my brother," Tamar protested. "Do not violate me, for such a thing is not done in Israel; do not do this disgraceful thing!" (13:12).

Tamar continued, "As for me, where could I get rid of my reproach? And as for you, you will be like one of the fools in Israel. Now therefore, please speak to the king, for he will not withhold me from you" (13:13).

But Amnon wouldn't listen. With his greater strength, he raped his half-sister.

Then Amnon hated Tamar with a greater hatred than his "love" had been. When his passion was satisfied, Amnon ordered his half-sister, "Get up, go away" (13:15).

Tamar protested. "No, because this wrong in sending me away is greater than the other that you have done to me!" (13:16).

However, Amnon wouldn't listen to her. He called for his young male attendant. "Now throw this woman out of my presence, and lock the door behind her" (13:17).

The attendant obeyed.

Tamar tore her varicolored, long-sleeved virgin's garment in the traditional Hebrew sign of mourning. She also put ashes on her head and went away crying.

Absalom, her full-brother, took her into his house and she remained there, desolate.

When King David heard what had happened, he was very

angry. But, as always with his sons, he did nothing. For a strong warrior and king, he was a very weak father.

Absalom didn't say anything to Amnon one way or another, but waited two years. At a dinner of the king's sons in Baal-hazor, near Ephraim, Absalom ordered his servants to kill Amnon. This was done.

The surviving princes fled on their mules. It was falsely reported to King David that all his sons had been massacred by Absalom. However, the king's nephew, Jonadab, who had plotted Amnon's rape of Tamar, corrected the report.

"Amnon alone is dead; because by the intent of Absalom this has been determined since the day that he violated his sister, Tamar" (13:32).

Absalom fled to safety with Talmai, the son of Ammihud, the king of Geshur, where he stayed three years. King David mourned for the dead first-born son and the fugitive killer, Absalom.

Nothing more is said of Tamar.

Although the Bible reports this case of incestuous rape, it has only been in recent times that people could talk openly of the significance of this tragedy.

Incest is apparently much more common than is generally believed. Reading the advice columns in the newspapers shows many women have sought help after an incestuous event. Interviews from former prostitutes who have become Christians show some began after an improper advance by siblings or father.

Without doubt, the forcing of sexual relations with a close relative invariably caused long-lasting (if not life-time) emotional scars. A form of self-loathing seemed inherent in such women.

Unfortunately, the Bible does not tell what happened to Tamar after her outward signs of grief and secluding herself. We don't know what reaction she had to the premeditated murder of her attacker by her full-brother.

We do know that the great King David did nothing except grieve for the dead and the exiled avenger.

No punishment was apparently ever meted out to the cousin, Jonadab, who cunningly suggested a violation of not only a beautiful virgin princess, but also of Israel's sacred laws.

Tamar, innocent of mind, unwittingly played into the hands of her half-brother, who plotted to take what he wanted without concern for the girl. Tamar, held fast in her stronger brother's grip, tried to reason with her assailant.

She pleaded that such a thing was not done in Israel. She begged her half-brother not to do the disgraceful thing. Then she appealed to Amnon's compassion by asking, "Where could I get rid of my reproach?" (2 Sam. 13:13).

Apparently that didn't ease Amnon's intentions, so Tamar appealed to his own self-interest. "You would be like one of the fools of Israel" (13:13).

The Scriptures do not describe the scene, but it seems logical that Tamar's seemingly-calm rationalizations were uttered in an increasingly violent physical situation. But still Tamar tried to reason with her attacker, saying as a last resort, "Please speak to the king, for he will not withhold me from you."

This proposal of marriage seems a violation of the ancient law summarized in Leviticus 18:11, "The nakedness of your father's wife's daughter, born to your father, she is your sister, you shall not uncover her nakedness."

Earlier, Abraham had been married to his half-sister, Sarah. By David's time, this was considered an incestuous relationship and forbidden. But perhaps the powerful David could have granted special dispensation to his children.

However, Amnon had no interest in marriage. He is said to have "loved" Tamar, but his behavior clearly demonstrates he had only unbridled self-gratification in mind.

So he raped his beautiful half-sister, threw her out of the house, and set in motion a chain of reactions that not only brought death to him, but also a continuous grief to his weak father.

The terrible aftermath of this incestuous rape continued for years. But we know nothing of the deep mental anguish that Tamar must have carried through the life not mentioned in the Scriptures.

We can imagine her anguished thoughts when she realized her logic wasn't going to work. We can believe how shocking an experience it was to come innocently and compassionately to aid her half-brother's illness, and then be seized with great strength! The horror she experienced in the explosive passion of her own half-brother can be visualized. Her remorse and shame can be imagined when her attacker's lust was spent and he ordered her away like a common prostitute.

Her early response to Amnon's demand suggests Tamar was able to think clearly. She pleaded with Amnon not to do such a disgraceful thing by sending her away. She asked him how she could ever again hold up her head in public. Sending her away would be a greater crime than what Amnon had just done, she explained.

But when Amnon threw Tamar out in disgrace, she tore her clothes and put ashes on her head. She sought seclusion with her full-brother, who urged her to be silent and not take the matter to heart.

It sounds as though Absalom, himself, didn't fully understand his sister's feelings of disgrace. But he was determined to take revenge, a violent act born of a violent act.

We must question how much of the terror and disgrace Tamar knew was her father's fault. Absalom planned vengeance on the attacker of his beautiful sister, but David, their father, was only angry. He did nothing. So the rape of Tamar released seeds of disgrace, revenge, and death. One moment of passion led to years of tragedy. In the end, we never learn what happened to Tamar, but we can safely assume she was emotionally scarred by incestuous rape and the vengeance that followed.

VASHTI
REFERENCES: Esther 1:9-19; 2:1, 4, 17
SCRIPTURAL SYNOPSIS:

Vashti was the beautiful queen of Ahasuerus, or Xerxes I. She lived about five hundred years before Christ in the kingdom of Persia. Her husband gave a royal feast while the queen entertained the visiting women in another section of the palace.

When the king had enjoyed his wine a week, he sent for his wife to show her off. She refused to come and was banished. Her vacant throne opened the way for Esther to become Ahasuerus's favorite.

COMMENTARY:

Persia (now Iran) had a despotic king who ruled over 127 provinces from India to Cush (Ethiopia) with the capital at Susa, or Shushan. The king showed off his riches for six months and then climaxed festivities by a seven day banquet. That's when Vashti enters the story.

The Scriptures say the king's palace court was the scene for the introduction of Vashti, his queen. The Jewish historian Josephus says the king had a tent pitched with supports of silver and gold. The tent was so immense that ten thousand visiting dignitaries could be seated at once. They were served from gold cups set with precious stones.

As a special consideration, Josephus adds, the king ordered that no guest was to be forced to drink "by bringing them wine continually, as is the practice of the Persians," but each guest was allowed to drink at his own pace.

However, after seven days, the princes, army officers, nobles, and other officials were obviously feeling no pain. The wine loosened inhibitions. The king called for Vashti "when merry with wine" (Esther 1:10).

The queen was entertaining women in another quarter of the palace when the word came. The king, her husband, wanted to show off her beauty to his guests. She was to wear her crown, the eunuchs concluded, giving the king's final word.

It is a scriptural diplomatic expression, for a footnote in Josephus explains that the king meant to present his wife nude.

The Scriptures simply say Vashti refused to come at the king's command. However, it is important to understand what extreme danger the queen had put herself in by refusing to obey the king.

He was a man of absolute authority except in one manner. If the law of the Medes and Persians was invoked, even the king could not revoke that law.

In the case of his throne room, both the Bible and Josephus show that anyone approaching the king unbidden was likely to be executed. Even the queen herself risked her life by such boldness, as the same story later proves. So when Vashti refused to come into the presence of the drunken king and his reveling cohorts wearing her royal crown and nothing else, she had committed an extremely grave breach of Persian custom.

The Scriptures do not explore Vashti's thoughts or feelings. The concentration is on the king's reaction. His counselors advised Ahasuerus to let it be written in the unrepealable laws of the Medes and the Persians that Vashti could come no more into the king's presence. The counselors warned that if the king didn't do that, all women would follow Vashti's example and become rebellious to their husbands.

But if the king deposed Vashti, the other women in the provinces would get the idea and stay in their places, the chief-prince and counselor advised the king.

The Bible says only that the king did as advised, but Josephus declares the king loved Vashti so much he suffered from the separation. However, under the law which couldn't be repealed, the king could not be reconciled to Vashti. His counselors then suggested finding virgins from which the king might take a new wife. This opened the way for the Jewish beauty, Esther, whose story is told elsewhere in the book.

Vashti probably would have been executed if she had not been so loved of the king. Josephus explains that the king kept royal headsmen, or axemen, beside his throne for prompt decapitation of those who dared oppose his rules. Therefore, Vashti emerges from the short scriptural account as a woman of uncommon bravery.

She was beautiful — exceeding all other women, according to Josephus — and she was queen, but she was subject to the despotic actions of her husband if she displeased him. Still, under the Persian law of her time, women were private people and not usually seen in public at all. So Vashti's refusal to be part of a drunken, nude display testifies to her high moral character and extreme bravery.

While the scriptural account is brief because the emphasis is on another woman, non-biblical sources show us Vashti as a woman of remarkable human traits. But the sources are so limited that an incomplete picture remains.

For example, the famous Greek historian, Herodotus, gives the queen's name as Amestris. Some scholars think the story of Vashti is mixed up with Artaxerxes II's wife, Stateira, who lived about fifty years later.

But one thing is certain: Vashti, whose cameo appearance in the Scriptures is only to pave the way for the Jewish heroine, Esther, was really quite a woman. She had everything, and yet she risked it all on her own moral principles. That's the human being who should be seen in the story of Vashti, the Persian queen who put principle even above life.

UNNAMED WOMEN
OF THE
NEW TESTAMENT

Some of the great stories in the New Testament feature nameless women. Some, like Peter's wife and mother-in-law, we'll never know more about than is now in the Scriptures. Others, like Herodias's unnamed daughter who danced before Herod, are known to us through Josephus, the Jewish historian. This secular writer even gives us this girl's name: Salome.

But most of those New Testament women who are nameless will remain so. Yet their stories are interesting because they tell us something more about the named people in the Scriptures. Sometimes we even learn something about the human traits of an unnamed woman.

So, while it is not possible to include every unnamed New Testament woman in our limited space, the following stories are used because of special interest or what there is to be learned of relevance today.

MOTHERS

PETER'S MOTHER-IN-LAW: This unnamed woman
was the mother of Simon Peter's wife, who is also unnamed.
(Matt. 8:14-15; Mark 1:29-31; Luke 4:38-39)

Peter's mother-in-law seems to have been nursed in her son-in-law's Capernaum home. She had a high fever that Jesus cured. This mother and mother-in-law promptly got up and served the Lord and His disciples.

This mother gave her daughter to a man who became one of Jesus' three closest disciples. And when this woman was able, she ministered to Him who had helped her. She didn't sit around and seek sympathy in recuperation.

The relevance is plain even for today: when Jesus touches a mother and mother-in-law, she should get up and do something practical for Him who has done so much for her.

JAIRUS'S WIFE: (Matt. 9:18-26; Mark 5:22-43; Luke
8:41-56)

This nameless mother has a minor part in the story, but we know she was in her home with mourners because her twelve-year-old daughter had died. The woman's husband, Jairus, had gone to get Jesus while the girl was sick and without knowing the child had died.

The mother's grief can be imagined. Her husband, a synagogue official, had been gone a long time. The mother naturally had no way of knowing that Jesus had started for their home when He was delayed by another woman in need.

The distraught mother's grief is evidenced in what had taken place since her husband went to seek Jesus' help. Jairus had been gone so long that even the flute players and noisy mourners were making a din. The place was in disorder. The crowd was scornful of Jesus' words of assurance upon arrival.

The mother and her husband alone of all that crowd were allowed into the room where Jesus spoke only a brief command: "Little girl, I say to you, arise!" (Mark 5:41). Luke tightens the command even more: "Child, arise!" (8:54).

The amazed mother and her husband saw their daughter restored to life. Jesus instructed that food be given her. And with the admonition to tell no one what had happened, the story ends.

But what of the mother? A few minutes before, she had been surrounded by a houseful of noisy, scornful mourners. We wonder what this mother said when she returned to the crowd with her living daughter at hand. The very human emotions of this mother are easily imagined as she hurried to feed her daughter and yet had to face Jesus' command to not tell what had happened.

It is a dilemma almost without equal, and leaves us with many unanswered questions. Yet few women in the Scriptures had more about which to rejoice than this nameless mother whose child was restored to life.

WIVES
PETER'S WIFE: Indicated clearly in 1 Corinthians 9:5 with the words, "Do we not have a right to take along a believing wife, even as the rest of the apostles, and the brothers of the Lord, and Cephas?"

Cephas, of course, is from the Greek word for "rock," Jesus' name for Simon Peter. We also know Peter was married because Jesus healed Peter's mother-in-law of a fever.

The Corinthians verse indicates all the apostles were married, including the Lord's brothers. But there is no firm evidence that the Corinthians verse literally meant every apostle and every one of the Lord's brothers. However, since the Hebrew language does not have a term for "bachelor," the literal interpretation of this passage is permissible.

PILATE'S WIFE: (Matt. 27:19)
She sent a message to her husband to have nothing to do with Jesus, who was then on trial before the Roman governor. Pilate's wife had experienced a disturbing dream over Jesus.

While apocryphal material has much to say about this woman, the Scriptures do not. Yet there is much to be gleaned from the few words.

In the same way that many important men today do not want

their wives to call them at the office, so the governor probably didn't care to receive his wife's message when he was sitting in judgment on a difficult trial. Yet she felt so strongly about her dream that she sent a messenger right into the courtroom.

The governor had just asked the unruly crowd, ''Whom do you want me to release for you? Barabbas, or Jesus who is called Christ?'' (Matt. 27:17).

Pilate's wife's message was brief but filled with caution and concern. She warned her husband to have nothing to do with ''that righteous Man.'' She gave her reasons. In her culture, dreams were still considered a source of reliable information.

The message apparently went unheeded. Matthew immediately continues his narrative by showing that the chief priests and elders persuaded the multitudes to demand Barabbas's release. The message of Pilate's wife was ignored, and the results, of course, were disastrous.

There is still relevance in this woman's life. When a wife cares enough, she risks warning her husband, even in the midst of official business. Pilate's wife had correctly judged Jesus' character. She tried and failed, but it is to her eternal credit that she tried to save an innocent Man.

However, as Jesus had said, His time had come. Nothing could stop the course of events in which Pilate was involved. His wife was a pivotal person in the world's greatest drama. Her ignored message still stands as a lesson in what might have been.

THE SAMARITAN WOMAN: (John 4:5-42)

Jesus had left Judea, heading north through Samaria to Galilee, when He encountered this woman at Jacob's well. Samaritans and Jews had nothing to do with each other (and hadn't for centuries). Yet Christ engaged this woman in a conversation which led to her believing in Him, and she helped many other Samaritans to accept Jesus as the Messiah.

She had been married five times, Jesus told her, and she was apparently illicitly living with her sixth man. The conversation was so unlikely that even Jesus' disciples ''marveled'' when they arrived on the scene.

Dialogue between Jesus and the Samaritan woman was brief, filled with symbolism and a discussion of their religious differences. Yet Jesus made His claims, plainly and simply. She went away believing and brought others to Jesus who also went away believing.

The lesson today is that even in a society that is morally deficient, with many people remarried and some even living together, Jesus did not condemn. He risked the disciples' surprise and perhaps displeasure to reconcile one woman to Himself. This despised Samaritan, to whom Jews wouldn't ordinarily have spoken, was open and receptive to Christ's message.

If we're not too quick to condemn, we may win Christian converts even among those considered by some to be inferior, and thereby win many others to the Lord. Jesus' message is above religious and cultural differences. His followers should learn something from this woman of Samaria.

SISTERS

In the New Testament, sisters seem largely to serve as fascinating flecks of humanity which help to flesh out the lives of principals like Jesus and Paul. Almost nothing is said about sisters, and yet their importance is indicated in their background roles.

Jesus, for example, had sisters. Paul had at least one sister. Mary, mother of Jesus, had a sister. Each of these played extremely brief, cameo roles in the Scriptures. Yet each contributed something to her more-well-known sibling. Jesus used sisters symbolically.

JESUS' SISTERS: (Matt. 13:56; Mark 6:3)

While four of Jesus' brothers are named (James, Joseph, Simon, and Judas), no sisters are named. There were at least two, according to both Matthew's and Mark's use of the plural.

Nothing specific is said about Jesus' sisters, but one of His comments shows how highly He regarded siblings.

Anyone who has left houses, brothers, sisters, father, mother, children, or farms ''for My name's sake'' would receive more, plus inheriting eternal life (Matt. 19:29).

A second comment followed word to Jesus that His mother and brothers were outside. Some manuscripts include "Your sisters." Jesus' reply was to look on all those sitting around Him and declare they were His mother and brothers. Jesus added, "For whoever does the will of God, he is My brother and sister and mother" (Mark 3:35).

Thus Jesus repeatedly made sisters of equal importance with other family members, although His own sisters are never mentioned by name in the Gospels. However, any woman today who does God's will automatically becomes Jesus' sister. So the lesson of relevance from the unnamed sisters in Jesus' childhood home is that those women who want to draw closer to Jesus today have only to obey God's will, and the relationship is established.

PAUL'S SISTER: (Acts 23:16-22)

Paul the apostle had an unnamed but married sister with at least one son, making Paul an uncle. While the Scriptures are mute in details of this sister's life, her importance in God's plan is made clear in reading between the lines.

Paul had recently stood before the high priest, Ananias, who had ordered the apostle struck on the mouth. As a heated discussion developed among the Jewish religious leaders, the chiliarch, or Roman commander in charge of a thousand troops, had removed Paul to the safety of the military barracks.

It was God's announced plan for Paul to witness in Rome. But a Jewish conspiracy developed to kill the prisoner when he was removed from Jerusalem.

Here's where God's sovereignty used Paul's sister. Because she was born and had a son, Paul's life was saved.

You'll remember that this unnamed sister's son heard of the plot and warned his uncle Paul, who sent the youth to the commander. Paul's life was spared and he went on to Rome to preach God's Word, according to God's plan.

But suppose Paul hadn't had a sister? Of course, God would undoubtedly have kept His servant, Paul, alive until His will through him had been accomplished. However, God used Paul's sister to produce a son who saved the great apostle's life.

Remember that even when it may seem that a sister is lost in the shadows of a brother's brighter life, nobody is unimportant to God. Everyone has a special role to play in God's greater plan. This is evident from Paul's sister, who probably had no idea her life was to give life to a son who would save Paul's life and help millions of people down through the centuries know something more of God's Truth, Way, and Life.

DAUGHTERS

As with daughters everywhere and in every time, there were good and bad female offspring in the New Testament times. We can consider some examples of these nameless daughters who represent good and evil.

PHILIP'S DAUGHTERS: (Acts 21:8-9)

These four virgins were the daughters of Philip the evangelist. Almost nothing else is said about them except they were prophetesses.

And that tells us a very great deal.

These women joined a very select number from the Old Testament and Anna of the Gospels who spoke by divine inspiration. The prophetesses — like their male counterparts of the Old Testament — spoke for God. God revealed His words to these special people who in turn told the multitudes what had been learned in personal, private revelation.

The prophetesses could not, therefore, be just ordinary women. Like Miriam, Huldah, and Deborah (Lapidoth's wife), they were intermediaries between God and man.

The very high regard God had for women in both the Old and the New Testaments is shown in His choosing to reveal secrets to those women who were somehow special, spiritually.

The Gospel writer's inclusion of the virginity of Philip's four daughters is obviously not for casual comment. The indication is that these women were above reproach in their personal lives. It is logical they had put Jesus first in their lives and were, in a spiritual sense, chosen brides.

They apparently still lived at home. Their father's high regard in the Scriptures shows his own spirituality and suggests the girls may have learned from him what values in life were greatest.

It is worth noting that the Old Testament prophetesses, Huldah and Deborah, were married. Miriam, sister of Aaron and Moses, has an unspecified marital status. Anna, as Luke points out, was a long-time widow of great age. It appears Philip's four virgin daughters were unique among their rare, very special counterparts.

There are many unanswered questions about these four unnamed women. Their mention is so brief, and only in Acts, that we wonder why the Holy Spirit moved Luke to include them. There can only be speculation. Their mention, however brief, speaks highly of their dedication to the service of Jesus Christ.

WIDOWS
THE NAIN WIDOW: (Luke 7:11-16)

There were no social agencies to sustain a widow in Jesus' time. Unless she had someone close, like a relative, the widow had to live on other people's leavings. In that sense, she was somewhat like today's big-city "basket women," those still-living but listless older discards of life who push their shopping carts through the streets, seeking an edible or partially useful bit of some more fortunate person's refuse.

There was nobody but God and the widow in some cases.

And so the Scriptures use these women to communicate great truths to we who live twenty centuries later.

Here are some of their stories:

Jesus was in Nain, a village some six miles from Nazareth in Galilee. Jesus had been ministering all around this area, but on this particular day he climbed the fifteen-hundred-foot hill to Nain.

He met the widow in a funeral procession.

Her husband was dead before Jesus met her. Now her only son was being carried out for burial. She was weeping, of course. Her friends accompanied her; a great number of them, indicating she was a good and popular woman.

Her emotions are not described because they are understood.

Jesus' feelings are plainly set down in the Gospel. He had compassion on her. He spoke only three words: "Do not weep" (Luke 7:13).

The Scriptures do not tell us the woman's reaction. We don't know if she recognized Jesus. We don't know if she felt a soaring hope at this Man. We don't know if she was offended by the intrusion on her grief. We only know that Jesus approached the bier and those carrying it stopped.

Jesus didn't make the woman suffer through the agony of not knowing who He was or what He was going to do. He spoke, "Young man, I say to you, arise!" (7:14).

The corpse was restored to life. The widow's son sat up, spoke, and Jesus "gave him back to his mother."

Nothing is said of the widow's emotions. But we can believe she joined those who began glorifying God. Word of the miraculous event reached beyond Nain in Galilee, past Samaria and throughout Judea to the south.

The widow of Nain is omitted from the Gospel after her son was restored to her. No more is said about how she felt or reacted. But her example lives today in the fact that she had lost both husband and son, but Jesus was coming her way. While there were many widows in the land, then as now, the widow is fortunate indeed because Jesus may be coming that woman's way, and there is hope, even in the presence of death.

SINFUL WOMEN
ADULTEROUS WOMAN: (John 8:1-11)

She had been caught in the act of adultery and brought to Jesus. The man involved was not mentioned, showing that the woman was to face stoning while her partner went free. But Jesus gave a masterful guideline for such cases and refused to condemn the woman. He sent her on with the admonition to "sin no more."

The woman's feelings can be understood. She was engaged in an illicit act. Her partner was not seized, yet she faced death. Her accusers set her in the middle of a group obviously hostile to her and to the One to whom they appealed for a decision. It was a test for Jesus, too.

The accusers cited the Law of Moses (Deut. 17:5-6) but asked for Jesus' comment. He wrote first on the ground and then told them: "He who is without sin among you, let him be the first to throw a stone at her" (John 8:7).

One by one, the accusers drifted away. Only then did Jesus ask, "Woman...will no one condemn you?"

"No one, Lord."

"Neither do I condemn you; go your way; from now on sin no more" (8:11).

The story is ended; but the woman's life had really just begun, assuming she heeded Jesus' words.

She had been brought to death's door. She had been reprieved by a few masterful words from Jesus to her accusers. She was not condemned even by the Son of God. There was only one condition: go, but sin no more.

The Scriptures declare all have sinned and fallen short. We can assume, it seems, that this greatly relieved woman went on to a new, vibrant life. But more than her story's truth is the lesson for today: Nobody is sinless. But when faced with Jesus Himself, there is no condemnation but only the commuting of a life sentence in the words, "Go...sin no more."

Heeding Jesus' words is better than a state governor's pardon at the eleventh hour.

WOMAN OF THE CITY: (Luke 7:36-50)

She was one of the nameless women of the streets. We can assume she was pretty, perhaps well-formed. She was obviously a prostitute. Yet when she heard Jesus was dining with Simon the Pharisee, she boldly entered the home and wordlessly began her adoration.

She stood behind Jesus as He reclined, in the Roman and Greek fashion of free men, at the low table. His bare feet stuck out behind Him. The woman didn't ask permission. She just did what she had come to do.

First, she wept. Penitent tears, no doubt. She allowed for rejection and ejection from Simon's home, but she wiped her tears off Jesus' feet with her own long tresses. She kissed those feet. She anointed them with perfume.

It is possible that the perfume had been purchased with the wages from her unsavory occupation. So far as the Scriptures are concerned, she was not condemned for that; it was her heart attitude that Jesus saw.

Naturally, the self-righteous host sniffed in disdain — not at her — but at Jesus, who didn't seem to know the woman's past. If Jesus was a prophet, the Pharisee reasoned, He would have known who the woman was.

Notice that there is no mention of the woman's thoughts. Yet in the tremendously incisive way the Holy Spirit has of writing concisely, we know the woman's emotions.

Jesus used the host's thoughts to tell a parable about forgiveness. The Guest involved His host in the response. The one who had the most to be forgiven would be the one who loved most. Then Jesus indicted His host with shortcomings compared to the strange woman. As a host, the Pharisee was inadequate compared to what this sinful woman had done.

Then Jesus spoke those beautiful words to the woman, "Your sins have been forgiven."

The woman's faith, demonstrated by an act of humble service, had saved her. She was to go in peace.

With that, the Scriptures end the story.

But for two thousand years, the ringing message has been declaring liberty to all who sin and take action to come to Jesus with penitent heart.

Everyone sins. Everyone needs to come to Jesus for His forgiveness. And, no matter what others say, the sincere act of faith sends the former sinner forth free of sin, saved by faith, and with peace in her heart and life.

It's good to remember this unnamed woman's relevant lesson after twenty centuries.

SYMBOLIC WOMEN

From the purity of Christ's bride to the mother of harlots in the Last Days, unnamed women in the New Testament represent the highest and the lowest traits of their sex. The allegorical use of unnamed women in the Gospels has given us lessons from two thousand years ago which are still timely as today — and even tomorrow.

For it is tomorrow that will bring understanding of the symbolic women in the book of Revelation (12:1-17), such as the woman, the dragon, and the child; the "great Harlot" associated with the mystery of Babylon the Great (17:1-18); and others, including the bride of Christ.

As with all representative stories Jesus told, women stand for a great truth which may not readily be understood. It is the parables that help separate those who have eyes but can't see and those having ears but who cannot hear.

Those truths are with us today, as fresh and meaningful as when Jesus first told them.

WOMAN WITH LEAVEN: (Matt. 13:33; Luke 13:21)

There is a sharp division among researchers on the subject of leaven, with some holding it to always mean evil. Other scholars see leaven as representing both good and evil. The latter seems to be the right interpretation of Jesus' parable on the subject.

To understand the story of the woman Jesus uses in both Matthew's and Luke's Gospels, it must be remembered what leaven was. Originally, a chunk of sour dough was saved from an existing mixture as a starter. The same comparison today might be made by women who make their own yogurt. In biblical times, leaven placed in a fresh dough caused fermentation and a resulting raised bread. Unleavened bread, specified in the Passover observance, was flat, having never had the time required to rise. In itself, the leaven was neither good nor bad.

Jesus used the example of leaven to demonstrate power and to help His listeners understand the Kingdom of heaven.

"He spoke another parable to them, 'The kingdom of heaven is like leaven, which a woman took, and hid in three pecks of meal, until it was all leavened'" (Matt 13:33).

It was in the woman's hands to influence the type of bread she was going to bake. She could have omitted the leaven with its power to raise the whole loaf, or add it. The choice was hers. In this case, the woman "hid" the powerful ingredient — small as it was — and it leavened the whole.

It is the same way with the Kingdom of God, Jesus pointed out. A small thing in hand, like a bit of leaven, could be used to influence the whole.

Detractors from this viewpoint recall that Jesus warned His disciples to "Beware the leaven of the Pharisees, which is hypocrisy" (Luke 12:1). But the comparison shows that in the hands of the unnamed New Testament woman, leaven was good and was something she could use to multiply what she had as a comparison to the Kingdom of heaven. The leaven of the religious leaders was to be avoided because it was incorrectly applied and produced adverse results.

The relevance of the parable of the leaven is plain today: even with a little power, a woman who properly uses it can have authority over much more and so be a part of the Kingdom of heaven.

THE TEN VIRGINS: (Matt. 25:1-13)

In another of His many discourses on the Kingdom of God, Jesus spoke of ten unnamed virgins with lamps. These women were equally divided among the foolish and prudent, for five took extra oil for their lamps before going to meet the bridegroom. The other five weren't properly prepared for the wait. When the bridegroom arrived unexpectedly, the unprepared women were locked out of the wedding feast.

The moral, as Jesus summarized it, was, "Be on the alert then, for you do not know the day nor the hour" (Matt. 25:13). While all the ten virgins had lamps, half of them didn't allow for the unexpected. In the end, the Bridegroom refused to admit the unprepared, saying, "I do not know you" (Matt. 25:12).

LAMB'S BRIDE/JESUS' BRIDE: (2 Cor. 11:2; Rev. 19:7; 21:2, 9; 22:17)

While some sources would suggest the book of Revelation's meaning or key to understanding has been lost, it is inconceivable that God would give us something without a purpose. Naturally, the purpose is to help us understand Him better. The spiritual significance of marriage in God's eyes is used as a symbol to show the fully prepared bride as the image of the true church.

Jesus is the Bridegroom. His prepared people are the bride.

Paul's imagery begins with his declaring that He had betrothed the church at Corinith as the virginal bride of "one husband, that to Christ" (2 Cor. 11:2). But in the same breath, the great apostle warns of his own fears: minds could be led astray as Eve was deceived by the devil personified as the serpent.

This beguiling but misleading temptation has obviously destroyed many bridal candidates in today's morass of religious confusion in which the simple and pure devotion to Christ has been subtly corrupted.

Revelation deals more deeply with the same symbolism of the Lamb's (Jesus') bride. In the first reference, rejoicing was proper because the bride was ready (Rev. 19:7). And she had made herself ready.

John's vision next deals with seeing the holy city, the new Jerusalem, coming down from God, "made ready as a bride adorned for her husband" (21:2). This symbolizes the absolute center of eternal bliss where the angels, God, and all His redeemed will gather after the judgment.

Notice that this high estate is represented as a bride adorned for her husband. This imagery is emphasized in Revelation 21:9. The final reference to the bride is in a direct quotation from Jesus just five verses from the end of the New Testament.

"I, Jesus, have sent My angel to testify to these things...and the Spirit and the bride say, 'Come.'"

With this invitation, the story of the Lamb's bride and the Holy City is concluded. We must now look at the ugly side of womenly imagery in the New Testament.

Since it is not the purpose of this volume to deeply probe every reference, only one distorted image of woman will be used.

MOTHER OF HARLOTS: (Rev. 17:1-18)

This entire chapter uses a harlot seated upon a scarlet-colored beast to represent a city called Babylon. The symbols represented by the beast and the harlot are to become reality in the coming days when the final battle between good and evil is waged.

It is this representation of a woman who is all that is wrong, evil, and wicked in the world. This "great harlot" (17:1) is the exact opposite of the virgin bride of the Lamb.

In both cases, women are used to represent the very highest and loftiest spiritual purity and the most low, base impurity possible. Yet as with the Lamb's bride, the "great harlot" is well-adorned. But this foul creature is clothed in purple and scarlet and gilded with gold, precious stones, and pearls. She holds a golden cup filled with abominations and unclean things of her immorality.

She does not operate alone, but sits on a scarlet beast with grotesque heads and horns. This fiendish woman and her nightmarish mount will war against Jesus, the Lamb.

But this woman's end is about as painful as can be imagined: eaten and burned. It is not a pleasant symbol because the Scriptures want to make a strong point.

Women in the New Testament represent the very highest and the very lowest imagery; that of the ready, adorned bride of Jesus; and that of the despicable depravity symbolized by a gilded harlot.

In each case, there is a human counterpart today as there was when John wrote his vision on the island of Patmos nearly two thousand years ago. The bride and the harlot both begin life as virgins. Faithfulness and purity make the bride a desirable woman; unfaithfulness and wantonness make the former virgin a totally undesirable woman whose end is predictably sad.

In an age of common immorality, such as marks the end of the twentieth century, the harlot is no longer held in such disrepute by many modern people. But in the timeless world of Jesus, the prospective Bridegroom, there is no change in viewpoint.

That's why the ancient symbolism of John's abominable woman as the great prostitute still represents all that is evil and impure.

Bride or prostitute: the Lord claims only the virginal; the harlot is destined to an ultimate end that places her as far from God as her choice of impurity made possible.

UNNAMED WOMEN OF THE OLD TESTAMENT

The parade of unnamed Old Testament women is long and fascinating. They range from young girls to old women. Their origins are often unknown. Their list of deeds is monumental.

While their names will never be known, the Scripture writers, acting under the guidance of the Holy Spirit, saw fit to tell us just enough of these women's stories to help us gain new insight into the reason they are mute witnesses to an ancient heritage which is ours today.

Here are some representative glimpses.

CAIN'S WIFE: (Gen. 4:17)

This is perhaps the most controversial woman in the entire Bible. For centuries, people have speculated on where she came from, ignoring Paul's warning to avoid subjects which are unprofitable.

As God never qualifies Himself, but simply states that He always was, so the Scriptures present Cain's wife as a fact, without providing any background.

She is mentioned only briefly in her role of conceiving Cain's son, Enoch. She is the first woman in the Bible after Eve, who had borne Cain. This first-born son had killed his younger brother and been banished to Nod, east of Eden.

One wonders how Cain's wife felt about being married to the world's first murderer. Perhaps she faced such doubts as knowing that since Cain had killed his own brother, might he also turn on his wife? Yet there is no indication of how Cain's wife felt, or thought, or reacted. She is pictured as a wife and mother, and then dropped from the scriptural narrative.

However, she bore a son whose name was given to the first city. The fact that there was such a thing as a city suggests many more people than the Scriptures identify.

It is from this second wife in the ancient days that a line of descendants came that included the first artistic types (musicians) and first craftsmen (ironsmiths).

Her humanity was fulfilled in being Cain's wife and a mother who gave, through her life, the foundation of that enduring cultural entity we call civilization.

WIDOW WHOSE SON WAS RESTORED TO LIFE: (1 Kings 17:8-24)

Elijah the Tishbite had warned King Ahab that there would not be any rain until the prophet said so. The Lord sent Elijah away to be fed by ravens until a brook dried up. Then the nameless widow's part is introduced.

God told the prophet to go to Zarephath near Sidon, where He had commanded a widow to provide for Elijah. But there was a different viewpoint expressed by the widow. She didn't seem to know anything about God's command. Therefore, the assumption is that God had planned to use her, although the only thing she really had to say about the situation was implied in her cooperative attitude.

When Elijah asked for water, even in the great drought that had driven him from the brook Cherith, the woman went to get the water. When the stranger asked for bread, the widow explained her problem.

She had none. There was a little flour and some oil with which she planned to make a last meal. Then she and her son would die.

As a human being, with emotions, doubts, and fears, this widow might have not heeded Elijah's next words. He promised that God would provide both flour and oil until it rained.

As a mother, the woman must have thought of her son. Should she dare give some of her son's final meal to a stranger who was saying God would provide beyond what her eyes could see?

The woman's faith is evident in her response. She obeyed Elijah. The flour and oil supplies remained constant. Seemingly, this would have made a complete story with a lesson, and the Scripture writers could have stopped.

However, another event is recorded. Her son fell sick and stopped breathing. The distraught widow and mother expressed her strong feelings to Elijah. The prophet took the child, prayed for his life to return, and the boy was restored.

It was only then, when her son was presented to her alive, that the widow expressed her certainty that "now I know that you are a man of God, and that the word of the Lord in your mouth is truth" (1 Kings 17:24).

The implication is that the woman had acted earlier on faith, not entirely sure that God's word was in the man to whom she offered hospitality. Yet, even in her earlier doubts, she had acted, and God had rewarded her. Only later was her faith firmly established because she had first acted on what faith she had.

POTIPHAR'S WIFE: (Gen. 39:6-20)

Among the many unnamed women of the Old Testament, Potiphar's wife may be chosen as the one most exhibiting selfishness and unbridled passion. She got Joseph in lots of trouble.

Joseph was a handsome Hebrew teenager, about seventeen, when his jealous brothers sold him into slavery. In Egypt, far from his Canaan homeland, Joseph was sold again to Potiphar. He was Pharoah's officer and captain of the bodyguard. The Lord was with the captive so that Joseph became successful, found favor in the captain's sight, and became Potiphar's personal servant and overseer of the house. Everything Potiphar owned was placed under the charge of young Joseph.

We can assume Joseph was a year or two older by the time all these achievements had been attained.

Then Potiphar's wife "looked with desire at Joseph, and said, 'Lie with me'" (Gen. 39:7).

It's logical to assume that Potiphar's wife was attractive. She was probably bored with her husband's being gone so much on his official duties to the Pharoah. She found the Hebrew slave attractive and wished to satisfy her desires by becoming unfaithful to her husband.

The Scriptures say "Joseph was handsome in form and appearance."

Potiphar's wife had everything she wanted, it seems, except Joseph. The single terse line in the Scriptures make her a very direct woman. "Lie with me" was plain enough. However, since she was not likely to invite rebuff as a first choice, she probably had already tried to seduce the handsome young Hebrew. When that didn't work, she spoke her mind.

What a surprise it must have been to hear Joseph refuse. "Behold," he explained logically, "with me around my master does not concern himself with anything in the house, and he has put all that he owns in my charge" (39:8).

It seems Joseph's explanation wasn't enough. Perhaps, Potiphar's wife was still doing something obviously sensual, for the slave felt the need to add some more words.

"There is no one greater in this house than I, and he has withheld nothing from me except you, because you are his wife. How then could I do this great evil, and sin against God?" (39:9).

Joseph had used a common-sense approach to an emotional problem. It didn't work. The spoiled, lonely Egyptian officer's wife didn't care about the rank her husband gave a male slave. She did not care that Joseph was a dependable, honorable, and moral man. Even though he was in a top management position, the woman did not care about Joseph's consideration of something he called "evil" and a sin against his God. That wasn't her concern. She wanted personal gratification. So she kept after Joseph.

Day after day, the Scriptures say, she spoke to Joseph. He didn't listen to her. He not only wouldn't sleep with her, but wouldn't even be with her.

We can see him walking out every time Potiphar's wife approached. We can see her planning to allure him with seductive clothing and perfumes. Her thoughts can be imagined. Joseph was a handsome young male, far from home, a slave who had no rights except what Potiphar gave him, and surely Joseph was in the prime of his manhood. Sooner or later, Potiphar's wife must have told herself, he'd give in.

But Joseph didn't. The woman's frustration grew over being scorned. Still, she wasn't quite ready to quit. One day, when Joseph was working in the house and none of the other men were around, Potiphar's wife made a physical advance.

She grabbed Joseph by his garment. "Lie with me!" It was a last desperate attempt by a passionate woman. Even her words have changed from the first, not in form or number, but in urgency and command. At first, she had probably said softly and seductively, "Lie with me," but now it's a direct command.

Joseph backed off so abruptly that the simple one-piece garment he was wearing remained in the woman's hand. He fled outside.

Potiphar's wife was left with her unsatisfied lust, her frustration, humiliation, anger, and Joseph's garment.

Potiphar's wife wasn't going to accept rejection without prompt vengeance against her reluctant male objective.

She called the men of the household, showed the garment Joseph had left in her clutch, and lied, blaming her husband for causing her a near rape by Joseph. "See, he has brought in a Hebrew to us to make sport of us; he came in to lie with me, and I screamed."

"And it came about when he heard that I raised my voice and screamed, that he left his garment beside me and fled, and went outside" (39:14-15).

Potiphar's inner anger had been well-masked from the witnesses she called. She had been the virtuous, valiant wife who resisted the unwelcome advances of a foreign slave. The way she told it, she was all things good and true.

Still, just to be sure, she kept the evidence beside her until her husband came home.

Then, as she had indicated to the household men, Potiphar was made to take the blame. She said to Potiphar, "The Hebrew slave, whom you brought to us, came in to me to make sport of me; and it happened as I raised my voice and screamed, then he left his garment beside me and fled outside" (39:17-18).

The Academy-Award performance of Potiphar's wife made her husband burn with anger, especially when she again goaded him with the suggestion that the whole thing was his fault, for "this is what your slave did to me."

The Scriptures drop Potiphar's wife at that point. Her story has been told. Potiphar obviously didn't care about the truth, or Joseph's story. Joseph was tossed in with political prisoners.

Potiphar's wife had many undesirable human attributes. These include unfaithfulness, since she had a husband; lust, since she wanted the handsome young Hebrew slave for an illicit affair. She was persistent, for she wouldn't give up easily. She was uncompassionate, since she didn't care about Joseph's rationale, his God, or his unjust punishment. Potiphar's wife was desperate, for she grabbed the slave's garment and held on so well that he was stripped of it in his efforts to escape.

When scorned, she proved herself a quick thinker and a good actress. She called in witnesses and exhibited evidence of her own virtuousness. She falsely claimed Joseph's disloyalty to Potiphar. She lied so cleverly, so convincingly, that Potiphar seems not to have even asked if Joseph had a side of the story. The woman had been absolutely convincing in her performance as the outraged wife who had successfully defended her honor.

In blaming Potiphar, she had put her husband in a spot where he could not equivocate. He had no choice. It was his slave, she said. She did it all so convincingly that she didn't even have to demand, "What are you going to do about it?"

She just told the "facts" as she saw them, and her woman's

intuition told her that Joseph would be punished without her having to suggest it.

So the Scriptures leave her after her last accusation against her husband, as though he was somehow involved in the alleged attack. Innocent Joseph spent a long time behind bars, but Potiphar's wife apparently escaped punishment.

But perhaps she was punished in other ways. Since each sin bears its own judgment, it may have been Joseph's absence that helped punish Potiphar's wife. The building of guilt that imprisons the mind might have brought further retribution to the Egyptian woman.

However, even if Potiphar's wife did escape earthly punishment for her sins, the Scriptures make it clear that she still faced God's eternal judgment.

On the other hand, Joseph's faithfulness to his God continued even behind bars, and he rose to become second only to Pharoah in all of Egypt.

The wife of Potiphar has left for us a relevant truth: The harvest of unbridled human desires and actions can be much more than imagined.

JEWISH SLAVE GIRL: (2 Kings 5:1-19)

She was a "little girl" from Israel who had been taken captive from Israel. The unnamed child was assigned to wait on the wife of Naaman, the leprous Syrian military commander. It is logical to assume that the girl was lonely, fearful, and even bitter. But the Scriptures give us a totally different picture.

It was common practice in her culture for marauders to seize wives and children and carry them off. Abraham rescued Lot's family after such an incident. David had the same kind of experience with his own wives being kidnapped. Even in Jesus' time, according to Josephus, it was not uncommon for the Romans to seize a whole village of Jews and sell them off for some real or imagined slight. The slave traders followed the Romans of Jesus' time, but in the case of this unnamed girl, it appears her captor simply handed her to his wife to be a slave-maid.

It would have been wise for the child to keep silent. But she expressed a thought that could have gotten her in deep trouble.

She said to her mistress, "I wish that my master were with the prophet who is in Samaria! Then he would cure him of his leprosy" (2 Kings 5:3).

The little girl had put her faith — and perhaps much more — on the line with that simple comment. She had reference to the prophet Elisha. He was a known miracle worker.

The unnamed Israelite girl could have been reprimanded by her mistress for suggesting a foreigner could do more for her husband than the Syrians. Worse, if the mistress got her husband to go see Elisha and he refused to help the attacker of his people, the girl's life might have been in jeopardy. Yet she seems so sure that she said her piece. Then the Scriptures say nothing more of her.

The viewpoint shifts to her mistress, who told her husband what the child had said. Naaman went to the Syrian king, who sent a letter to the king of Israel. He was greatly distressed. But Elisha heard of the case, had his king send word back to Syria, and the leprous Naaman arrived with horses and chariots and a lot of vanity to be cured. After some displays of his haughtiness, he obeyed Elisha and was cured. But Naaman's leprosy was transferred to Behazi, Elisha's lying servant.

All this presumably would have made the Syrian military commander return in gratefulness to his wife's captive maid. However, nothing is said about her. Her part was done. She had faith in the man of God. She helped an enemy who became a believer in the little girl's God (5:17).

This unnamed slave girl became a living example of those great principles of humanity that Jesus expounded so clearly several hundred years later.

We don't know her name, but we know this girl's human heart. And her example stands before us today as a guide to what God can do even for an enemy when we're moved by compassion.

WITCH OF ENDOR: (1 Sam. 28:6-25)

The Scriptures call her a medium, or one with a familiar spirit, but the general acceptance of her role is that of witch. Her story is one of the most intriguing in all the Old Testament because it gives a bizarre glimpse of life after death.

She is introduced after King Saul's behavior had separated him from God. He would not answer Saul in any of the usual ways. So Saul ordered his servants to find a medium with a familiar spirit so he could inquire of her.

When word was brought to Saul that there was such a woman at En-dor, a village about half a dozen miles southeast of Nazareth, the king disguised himself and approached the woman.

Her suspicious nature is shown in her citing the violation of the king's law for calling up someone from the dead. Saul assured her there would be no punishment. Then the woman agreed to do as the disguised king asked.

The prophet Samuel had been dead for some time. Yet when Saul asked her to "conjure up for me... Samuel" (28:8, 11), she did.

The woman saw Samuel and immediately realized who her disguised night visitor was. She was obviously very much afraid for her involvement.

The king reassured her and asked an interesting question, "What do you see?" (28:13). Apparently Saul could not see the visitor from the dead.

The woman replied, "I see a divine being coming up from the earth." An alternative reading of the figure is "a god."

Saul still couldn't see the figure. The woman described him as an old man wrapped with a robe. Saul recognized the description and bowed to the ground in homage. But Saul did have a conversation with the famous prophet who had been recalled from beyond the grave.

The woman heard the conversation. Samuel reprimanded Saul for disturbing him. Saul explained his reasons. Samuel pronounced disaster upon the king for not obeying God.

The Scriptures do not say how Samuel or his form left. Saul's reaction is recorded, however, and the woman's response.

She had obeyed Saul against the law's opposite orders. She had risked her life. Now she wanted to give Saul some advice. She wanted to make him something to eat since Saul was faint from hunger and from fright.

She persisted, had a calf slaughtered, and she made bread. When she had served him, Saul and his servants went into the night.

Nothing more is said about the woman who was a medium. Her story remains one of the most awesome in the Bible, and her human traits among the most interesting.

First, she was in violation of the king's law; when Saul came to her, she was cautious and suspicious. She had amazing powers not specifically detailed in any other woman recorded in the Scriptures. She was witness to a strange sight and conversation because of what she had done. Yet in the end, this woman showed compassion and concern and demonstrated hospitality for her frightened guest.

Because of her illegal activities, she must be listed among the infamous women of the Bible. She demonstrated a strange power beyond human comprehension: the calling up of the dead.

Her human traits suggest an earlier life against not only the king's law but also against God's. She was afraid as all should be who break the commands of government and Lord. Yet there is something in her final scriptural acts which suggest that perhaps the horrible event in which she had participated somehow changed her, and she was compassionate to a man who had disobeyed God and was soon to die along with his sons.

It may be wishful thinking, but it is possible that even this strange woman with dark powers might have ended her life as a better person than the way she is generally remembered: the witch of Endor.

Bibliography

Davis Dictionary of the Bible. Grand Rapids, Mich.: Baker, 1972.

Miller, Madaleine S., and Miller, J. Lane. *Harper's Encyclopedia of Bible Life.* New York: Harper, 1978.

Deen, Edith. *All the Women of the Bible.* New York: Harper, 1955.

Harrison, R.K. *Old Testament Times.* Grand Rapids, Mich.: Eerdmans, 1974.

Pfeiffer, Charles F. *Baker's Pocket Atlas of the Bible.* Grand Rapids, Mich.: Baker, 1973.

Comay, Joan. *Who's Who in the Old Testament.* New York: Holt, Rinehart, and Winston, 1971.

Halley, Henry H. *Halley's Bible Handbook.* Grand Rapids, Mich.: Zondervan, 1975.

Alexander, David, and Alexander, Pat, eds. *Eerdmans Handbook of the Bible.* Grand Rapids, Mich.: Eerdmans, 1973.

Lockyer, Herbert. *All the Women of the Bible.* Grand Rapids, Mich.: Zondervan, 1967.

Tenney, Merrill C., ed. *The Zondervan Pictorial Encyclopedia of the Bible.* Grand Rapids, Mich.: Zondervan, 1977.

Kuyper, Abraham. *Women of the New Testament.* Grand Rapids, Mich.: Zondervan, 1934.

Cruden, Alexander. *Cruden's Complete Concordance.* Grand Rapids, Mich.: Zondervan, 1949.

Taylor, Kenneth. *The Living Bible.* Wheaton, Ill.: Tyndale, 1971.

Alexander, Pat, ed. *Eerdman's Family Encyclopedia of the Bible.* Grand Rapids, Mich.: Eerdmans, 1978.

Everyman's Atlas of Ancient and Classical Geography. New York: Dent, 1975.

General References

Bahant, Dan. *Carta's Historical Atlas of Jerusalem*. Jerusalem: Carta, The Israel Map and Publishing Co., 1973.

Dimont, Max I. *The Indestructible Jews*. New York: Signet Books, New American Library, 1971.

Dimont, Max I. *Jews, God and History*. New York: Signet Books, New American Library, 1962.

Ginzberg, Louis. *The Legends of the Jews*. New York: Simon & Schuster, 1953.

Golden, Judah. *The Living Talmud*. New York: Mentor Books, New American Library, 1957.

Graetz, H. *History of the Jews*. Vol. 2, Philadelphia: Jewish Pub. Soc. of Amer., 1971.

Great People of the Bible and How They Lived. Pleasantville, N. Y.: Reader's Digest, 1971.

Gromacki, Robert G. *New Testament Survey*. Grand Rapids, Mich.: Baker, 1977.

Jacobs, Louis. *Jewish Law*. New York: Behrman, 1968.

Josephus: Complete Works. Translated by William Whiston. Grand Rapids, Mich.: Kregel, 1978.

Keller, Werner. *The Bible as History*. Translated by William Neil. New York: Morrow, 1956.

Kertzer, Morris N. *What Is a Jew?* New York: Macmillan, 1965.

McDowell, Josh. *Evidence That Demands a Verdict*. San Bernadino, Cal.: Campus Crusade, 1972.

Miller, Madelaine S., and Miller, J. Lane. *Harper's Bible Dictionary*. New York: Harper, 1952.

Slaughter, Frank G. *The Galileans*. New York: Doubleday, 1977.

Steinberg, Milton. *Basic Judaism*. New York: Harcourt, 1947.

Terrien, Samuel. *The Golden Bible Atlas*. Racine, Wis.: Western, 1957.

Williamson, G. A. *The World of Josephus*. New York: Little, Brown, 1964.

Wouk, Herman. *This Is My God*. New York: Pocket Books, 1973.

Great Religions of the World. Washington, D.C.: Nat. Geog. Soc., 1971.

CHRISTIAN HERALD ASSOCIATION AND ITS MINISTRIES

CHRISTIAN HERALD ASSOCIATION, founded in 1878, publishes The Christian Herald Magazine, one of the leading interdenominational religious monthlies in America. Through its wide circulation, it brings inspiring articles and the latest news of religious developments to many families. From the magazine's pages came the initiative for CHRISTIAN HERALD CHILDREN'S HOME and THE BOWERY MISSION, two individually supported not-for-profit corporations.

CHRISTIAN HERALD CHILDREN'S HOME, established in 1894, is the name for a unique and dynamic ministry to disadvantaged children, offering hope and opportunities which would not otherwise be available for reasons of poverty and neglect. The goal is to develop each child's potential and to demonstrate Christian compassion and understanding to children in need.

Mont Lawn is a permanent camp located in Bushkill, Pennsylvania. It is the focal point of a ministry which provides a healthful "vacation with a purpose" to children who without it would be confined to the streets of the city. Up to 1000 children between the ages of 7 and 11 come to Mont Lawn each year.

Christian Herald Children's Home maintains year-round contact with children by means of an *In-City Youth Ministry.* Central to its philosophy is the belief that only through sustained relationships and demonstrated concern can individual lives be truly enriched. Special emphasis is on individual guidance, spiritual and family counseling and tutoring. This follow-up ministry to inner-city children culminates for many in financial assistance toward higher education and career counseling.

THE BOWERY MISSION, located at 227 Bowery, New York City, has since 1879 been reaching out to the lost men on the Bowery, offering them what could be their last chance to rebuild their lives. Every man is fed, clothed and ministered to. Countless numbers have entered the 90-day residential rehabilitation program at the Bowery Mission. A concentrated ministry of counseling, medical care, nutrition therapy, Bible study and Gospel services awakens a man to spiritual renewal within himself.

These ministries are supported solely by the voluntary contributions of individuals and by legacies and bequests. Contributions are tax deductible. Checks should be made out either to CHRISTIAN HERALD CHILDREN'S HOME or to THE BOWERY MISSION.

Administrative Office: 40 Overlook Drive, Chappaqua, New York 10514
Telephone: (914) 769-9000

Date Due